Warton in Wartime

Harry Holmes

Other Tempus Aviation Titles include:

Airships of the First World War	Terry C. Treadwell
Auster	Ken Wixey
Avro	Harry Holmes
Avro Anson	Harry Holmes
Avro 748	Harry Holmes
Beechcraft	Ken Wixey
The Blackburn Aircraft Company	Malcolm Hall
Blériot: Herald of an Age	Brian A. Elliot
Boeing	Martin Bowman
Boulton Paul Aircraft	The Boulton Paul Association
Bristol Aeroplane Company: A History	Alec Brew
Britten Norman	George Marsh
A Century of Flight	John W. R. Taylor
Comet & Nimrod	Ray Williams
In Cornish Skies	Peter London
De Havilland Aircraft Company	Maurice Allward & John Taylor
In Dorset Skies	Colin Cruddas
The Douglas Skymaster Family	Ken Wixey
Dowty And The Flying Machine	Derek N. James
The English Electric Lightning	Martin W. Bowman
Fairey Aviation	John W. R. Taylor
Filton and the Flying Machine	Malcolm Hall
Gloster Aircraft Company	Derek N. Jones
Grumman TBF Avenger	Martin W. Bowman
Handley Page	Alan Dowsett
Hawker Aircraft	Derek N. James
Ironworks: The Story of Grumman Aircraft	Terry C. Treadwell
Lockheed	Martin W. Bowman
The Lockheed Constellation	Ken Wixey
Lufthansa	Mike Hooks
Miles Aircraft	Rod Simpson
Napier Powered	Alan Vessey
P51 Mustang	Harry Holmes
Parnall's Aircraft	Ken Wixey
Percivals Aircraft	Norman Ellison
Piper Aircraft	Rod Simpson
Richthofen's Flying Circus	Terry Treadwell & Alan Wood
Royal Flying Corps	Terry Treadwell & Alan Wood
Shropsire Airfields	Alec Brew & Barry Abraham
Sopwith Aviation Company	Malcom Hall
Spirit of Hamble: Folland Aircraft	Derek James
Vickers Aircraft	Norman Barfield
Waco	Rod Simpson & Charles Trask

WARTON IN WARTIME

Harry Holmes

TEMPUS

First published 2001
Copyright © Harry Holmes 2001

Tempus Publishing Limited
The Mill, Brimscombe Port,
Stroud, Gloucestershire, GL5 2QG

ISBN 0 7524 2120 4

Typesetting and origination by
Tempus Publishing Limited
Printed in Great Britain by
Midway Clark Printing, Wiltshire

Contents

Acknolwledgements

My grateful thanks must go to members of the BAD2 Association for thier generous help with the photographic coverage in this book. Many who assisted have now passed on, but thier contributions formed an important part of this tribute to *Warton in Wartime*.

Cover Photo:
One section of Warton's Alert Crew posing with an A-26 Invader in April 1945.
Rear row (L to R), Byron Amundson; Eddie Kamody; Lt Tom Flowers (Section Leader) and gordon Fellow.
Front row, Paul Oberdorf and Arthur Malow.

Introduction

After the outbreak of the Second World War it was obvious that the need for airfields would take on a greater urgency and any sites previously rejected would have to be reassessed. One such site was Freckleton Marsh, near Lytham St Annes on the Lancashire coast, which had been surveyed by the Air Ministry in 1936 but was found to be unsuitable for an aerodrome. Known locally as Grange Farm, the area came under scrutiny once more but with yet another rejection. However, just half a mile along the coast towards the village of Warton, the ground was much more stable. In 1940 work commenced on the site to construct an airfield for the RAF as a satellite for the nearby Squires Gate aerodrome where detachments of a number of fighter and bomber units were already located. The decision to build the airfield delighted the local Fylde Rural Council although a number of poultry farmers greeted the news with anger as their farms would have to make way for the aerodrome.

In October 1941 the British Government was approached by the United States with a request for suitable sites in Britain for possible use as air depots for the United States Army Air Force (USAAF). Four airfields were proposed, with these being named as Little Staughton near Bedford, Langford Lodge in Northern Ireland and Burtonwood and Warton, both in Lancashire. At that time work was already underway at Burtonwood on the overhaul and repair of American-built aircraft serving with the RAF but with the entry of the United States into the war in December 1941 there was a requirement for these facilities to be operational as soon as possible. The urgency became acute with the announcement that the USAAF planned to have 1,000 aircraft operating from bases in Britain by August 1942 and over 3,500 by mid-1943.

In May 1942 an agreement was finalised to transfer Burtonwood to the exclusive control of the Americans, following an interval of joint working keeping the British staff already located there. This joint venture ended much sooner that expected as, by the end of the following month, the base was under the full control of the   US 8th Air Service Command (AFSC). After the departure of the British specialists it was found that there was a shortage of skilled technicians amongst the US military personnel requiring American civilian engineers to be brought in from the United States to fill the gap. The 8th AFSC was part of the United States 8th Air Force which had been activated at Savannah, Georgia on 28 January 1942 and then selected to establish the USAAF in Britain on 8 April 1942.

The construction of Warton and Langford Lodge, with the many facilities required by an air depot, had fallen well behind schedule, which meant that Burtonwood was the sole operational air depot. It was then decided that the depot in Northern Ireland would have limited capability to support the large number of combat groups which were to be based in East Anglia and the East Midlands. Priority was then given to Little Staughton, which was designated as a Strategic Air Depot (SAD) as it would be located nearest to the 8th Bomber Command's operating area.

This change of emphasis on the air depot programme would mean that now only Burtonwood and Warton would concentrate on heavy maintenance, while Langford Lodge would devote its efforts to various modifications and engineering research.

Bomber aircraft had started to be flown into Britain while the fighter types came by sea to either Liverpool or Glasgow, fully cocooned but minus propeller, ailerons, wingtips and tail assembly, which were boxed.

P-38 Lightnings and later, P-61 Black Widows, arrived without their outer wings. The smaller fighters were towed through the streets of Liverpool on RAF low-loaders, while the twin-engined machines were pulled by tractor units using the aircraft's own undercarriage. The aeroplanes were then assembled at Speke airport before being flown, while the Glasgow arrivals received similar treatment at Renfrew. Once the air depots had been established the aircraft were delivered to them for inspection and any modifications before eventually going to a combat unit.

It was on 18 August 1942 that the first contingent of Americans arrived at Lytham railway station, which was just four miles from Warton aerodrome. These would be the first of many and the whole north west of England would soon begin to feel the impact of their arrival in the area. The troops arriving at Warton would soon be working very hard to get the base established and fully operational, but the possibility of playing hard too, was not lost on the Americans as the delights of Blackpool were only a few miles away.

On 5 September 1942 the name of the Warton Air Depot was established by order of the 8th AFSC, after originally being planned as the 402nd Air Depot. The reason for the station's existence soon became clear as aircraft began to arrive in large numbers, both new and operational types, including battle damaged aeroplanes. The latter would have to be repaired and, in some cases, whole sections were rebuilt or replaced. Any beyond repair went to the salvage section which would relieve the aircraft of any usable part for storage or incorporation into other machines. The requirements of an air depot called for every type of technical skill on the full range of aircraft which would eventually arrive in the European Theatre of Operations (ETO). Also needed were the means of flying the aircraft from other locations into Warton and, after processing, delivering them to their own base or other airfields. This task was originally undertaken by the 87th Air Transport Squadron, a detachment of the 27th Air Transport Group based at Heston, Middlesex. The 87th also had sections at Burtonwood and Langford Lodge. The steady increase in air traffic, from both ferrying and the primary rôle of air transport, was overwhelming the Squadron, resulting in the arrival of the 310th Ferrying Squadron. The 310th became responsible for all ferrying duties, leaving the 87th free to continue its air transport work.

On 12 February 1943 the facility's name changed from Warton Air Depot to Army Air Force (AAF) Station 582 for security reasons, but it would be 17 July 1943 before the station was handed over from the RAF to the United States. A large parade to mark the occasion took place on the parking ramp in front of the main hangars. Once the ceremony had ended the smartly turned out troops quickly changed into their overalls for the return to duty.

As Warton's personnel gained experience the unit started to meet its production targets after the slow progress on the development of the site. The aircraft processing had not commenced in earnest until April 1943 and it was not until July of that year that the first statistical report was issued. Aircraft had been passing through the depot but these were new aeroplanes arriving for inspection only before clearance to their assigned units. These machines did not feature in the production figures and it was August 1943 before any actually appeared, with just three B-17s having extensive modification work before their delivery. After some delay, the first real task was for the installation of external release switches for the life-raft compartment, modification of radio and intercom equipment and the enlargement of ammunition boxes on B-17s. Because so many sections were involved in this work it became apparent that a drastic rationalization of the departments within the unit would be needed.

The production expansion as the USAAF's build-up continued meant that the busiest section at Warton was bound to be Flying Control. A small detachment of men belonging to the 7th ADG arrived after gaining some air traffic control experience from the RAF and a full-time Flying Control Unit was established in February 1943 using both American and British controllers. Their equipment was extremely basic, consisting of two Very pistols, one Aldis lamp and a very old radio set but, as the volume of flying increased, priority orders for additional and much-needed supplies of communications equipment began arriving. The installation of runway lighting was a great help allowing flight operations to continue over longer periods. The first real excitement for the new Flying Control came early in May 1943 when a flight of B-17s arrived in the circuit. All had gone well until one pilot reported that he could not lower his wheels and he was advised to circle the airfield until arrangements could be made for an emergency landing. A controller drove a jeep down the airfield laying out coloured streamers on the grass to guide the bomber for a belly-landing on the safest part of the field. The pilot made a dry run over the grass and continued to circle Warton before making a good approach and promptly setting the Fortress down on its belly in the middle of the main runway, bringing the day's flying to an abrupt halt! The RAF personnel stayed in Flying Control at Warton until 9 December 1943 when, much to their sadness, they were posted away to RAF stations leaving the USAAF people in complete control of flight operations.

Military personnel continued to arrive at Warton at an amazing rate. Due to the shortage of accommodation a 'tent city' was set up using large bell-tents and it was unfortunate for many of the troops that they had to spend the winter of 1943-1944 under canvas.

It was on 21 October 1943 that Warton's title was changed once more, as AAF Station 582 became known as Base Air Depot (BAD) No.2 when it became part of the newly established Base Air Depot Area (BADA) Command. Besides the new title the arrival of a new Commanding Officer and other senior ranks prompted a new enthusiasm which contributed greatly to station morale with the motto 'It can be done' being adopted by BAD.2. This would prove to be true as the station went on to break many production records in terms of aircraft processed and delivered to active units.

With the new area command structure Burtonwood became BAD.1, while Langford Lodge was known as BAD.3. However, the constant flow of aircraft from the United States put a great strain on the air depots. Besides new aircraft, numerous modifications were required by the combat units for missions in the ETO, regular inspections and, of course, battle damage repairs, with all of these forcing both Burtonwood and Warton to introduce around the clock working. Before the end of 1943 these two sites had their workloads increased as medium bombers and transports started to arrive in addition to the heavy bombers and fighters. The need for rationalization became even more urgent, with the first changes coming in the engine overhaul sections at the air depots. In December 1943 it was ordered that all radial engines would be processed at BAD.1 while in-lines would be assigned to BAD.2 instead of the mixture of engine types then currently being worked upon. BAD.3 at Langford Lodge would manufacture repair kits and also repair electrical propellers. At Warton, Hangar Nos 1 to 5 would eventually be for production while Nos 6 and 7 would be for Flight Test.

Combat requirements amongst the aircraft types too were changing as experience was gained in the air battle over Europe, but it was the need for additional firepower, armour plating, better vision and a host of other improvements which added to the air depots' work programmes. As the expansion continued, rationalization of the bases was also introduced, with BAD.1 taking the lion's share of B-17s, P-38s and P-47s, while BAD.2 at Warton would specialize in the B-24 Liberator and the newly arriving P-51 Mustangs. Each station would take various types as required and, because of the pressure, BAD.3 was brought into the equation to modify some B-17s and P-38s. The build-up of the US 9th Air Force, which was re-formed in England after serving in North Africa, would add to the aircraft quota, with the obvious forthcoming invasion. The 9th Air Force had been servicing its own fighters, but the arrival of A-20 Havocs, B-26 Marauders and C-47 transports at the air depots added to their great burden. Assembly of liaison aircraft, such as the L-4 Grasshopper and L-5 Sentinel, would eventually become the responsibility of the BADs.

As the aircraft specialization was coming into effect at the BADs, large-scale rationalization was also underway with the various units serving at the bases. Many sections were inactivated, with personnel and equipment being absorbed into newly created divisions, the largest of these being the Maintenance Division, with Supply and Administration making up two more. The Maintenance Division fully encompassed Warton's mission plan, as the Aircraft Section,

Manufacture and Repair, Production Inspection and Planning, Assessories Section and the Engine Repair Department came under it. The Aircraft Section, of course, included Flight Test.

By November 1943 a total of 1,216 aircraft had been delivered from Warton and, although the majority of them had been new arrivals from the United States, only being cleared after inspection and flight test, 119 of them had been fully processed by BAD.2. The rationalization programme would greatly increase this figure in the months to come.

By the end of 1943 the new P-51B Mustangs were appearing in great numbers and work had commenced to familiarize personnel with all aspects of the fighter. Almost immediately problems started to arise with a shortage of radiator gaskets, but this trouble was relieved by the ingenuity of the BAD.2 engineers who devised an excellent substitute by using a rubber composite material which could be adapted for the purpose. This method was cleared for use in the field by the aircraft's manufacturers, North American Aviation.

The turn of the year saw the completion of the engine overhaul change-over, with personnel attending the In-Line Engine School which was staffed by technical representatives from Allison and Rolls-Royce with the latter's Merlin engine starting to arrive at Warton from the original manufacturer and from the United States where Packard Motors built it under licence. Before the change Warton's engine mechanics had overhauled 126 radials before all materials and some specialists were transferred to BAD.1 at Burtonwood, while the scheme saw in-line engine equipment travelling in the opposite direction.

With the main aircraft types starting to be allocated to their specialist units the appearance of other new types was already planned and would add to the work programmes. It was decreed that the forthcoming A-26 Invader medium bomber would be processed by BAD.2 at Warton, as it was to replace the A-20 Havoc already being overhauled there, while the large P-61 Black Widow night fighter would be assigned to BAD.1. The large numbers of C-47 transport aircraft would be shared between the depots.

From the beginning of January 1944 until the end of the war, BAD.2 was working at full capacity and it was on the 16th of that month that the first Packard-built Rolls-Royce Merlin was run in the Engine Test Block without a hitch. The sheet metal workers of the Manufacturing and Repair Department were presented with an important task as orders were issued by BADA that special jigs and tools had to be manufactured to completely rework the main spar of P-51 tailplanes. From 9 January until 1 March 300 P-51 Mustangs were processed, turned over to Flight Test, flown without one technical failure and cleared to be ferried to combat units.

On 21 March a further directive was received concerning the P-51 at Warton. This time it was ordered that every engine bolt would have to be removed and tested to determine the correct tensile strength before being X-rayed to detect any minute cracks. Any replacement bolts had to be manufactured on site.

The accommodation and office building programme had been progressing through the winter and by March 1944 several new buildings were occupied. After a tour of inspection it was ordered that the Internal Supply Section should vacate Hangar No.1 to make way for additional space required for aircraft and within twelve hours the whole branch was moved to two new large warehouses which had been erected on the opposite side of the main road, which ran from Lytham to Preston.

The strength of the depot continued to increase as by the beginning of March personnel totalled 10,408, but this was reduced by 1,200 by the middle of that month with the transfer of men to AAF Station 594 at Stone in Staffordshire. However, the move had been caused by an administrative error and most of the troops returned to BAD.2 by the end of the month.

During April it was announced that a War Bond Drive would commence with a target of $114,000 to purchase two P-51 Mustangs. Amazingly, the drive was oversubscribed with enough money collected from the base personnel to buy a third Mustang.

In the middle of May 1944 Warton received a visit from Lieutenant General James H. Doolittle. This tour of the station was not an official visit but more of a Public Relations exercise and he went out of his way to meet as many of the BAD.2 personnel as time allowed. This proved to be an unforgettable experience for those lucky enough to chat to the legendary Jimmy Doolittle.

By the end of May all of the anti-aircraft guns that ringed the base, as well as the sole gun which was located on the ramp opposite to Hangar No.2, disappeared to a location in southern England. It was later found that they would take part in the invasion of Europe.

Probably the most famous aircraft to come out of Warton was a P-51B Mustang by the name of *Spare Parts*. It had arrived at Liverpool docks in February 1944 but was dropped while being unloaded and classed as a write-off, with the remains being transported to Warton to be used as spares. The Warton engineers requested that they be allowed to rebuild the aircraft in their own time and permission was granted providing that the work was officially inspected at every stage. The Mustang eventually took shape and reached the flying stage by the end of May with further permission being received to fly the aeroplane, providing that it would not be delivered to a combat unit but stay at BAD.2 as a 'hack' aircraft. The command radio set was removed from behind the pilot's seat and a passenger seat installed. The aircraft soon began to justify all the effort of the rebuild as it allowed mechanics to fly in a single-engine fighter plane, but its real importance came as the station's whisky runner! An arrangement was made with a Scottish distillery and, as no guns were fitted, the gun compartments made ideal storage space for quite a number of bottles. The flight to Scotland was made on a regular basis and probably did more for morale than any other single factor. Sadly, the aircraft was lost in an accident late in 1944. However, official records state that the machine was 'damaged beyond repair at Liverpool on 20 February 1944'. The majority of the P-51s unloaded that day went to the famous 4th Fighter Group at Debden, Essex and perhaps, without the accident, *Spare Parts* could have become the mount of one of the famous aces. However, the personnel at BAD.2 were convinced that even in her short life that Mustang did more for the war effort than many of her sisters ever did!

Operation 'Overlord', which took place on 6 June 1944, was the largest combined operation the world had ever witnessed. The air forces had to play a vital role covering the landing forces and attacking heavily defended targets on the French coast. The vast scale of 'Overlord' required continuous support, nowhere more-so than at the Base Air Depots. News of the landings was announced over Warton's tannoy system and every man felt that he would have to work just that little bit harder. The steady increase in the turnover rate for the first five months of 1944 was encouraging and the result of their efforts was reflected by the 8th and 9th Air Forces having aircraft in reserve. The need for these aircraft came shortly after D-Day and in the following months the Aircraft Departments at the BADs were taxed to the utmost. The uncertainty of the English weather was always in the minds of any aircrew, but for the pilots of Flight Test it became necessary to test fly over 800 aircraft in the month of June. Some of these required two or more flights before they could be cleared for release to the combat units. Because some days were lost through bad weather, as many as fifty test flights had to be carried out in a single day. Considering that there were only ten pilots available this was a magnificent achievement.

One of the most difficult tasks during that period fell to the Alert Crew who had the responsibility for servicing and dispersing aircraft around the airfield and maintaining all cleared machines in a 'ready' state, which meant daily and pre-flight inspections. With a small number of aircraft this would have been an easy task, but with 800 aircraft on the airfield sometimes, with 300 of those ready for delivery, it called for the highest degree of competency. Great skill and care was needed in the handling of aircraft to avoid damage to others in the tightly packed parking areas.

In conjunction with all this activity, Air Traffic Control in Warton's tower (call-sign, 'Farum'), accomplished an outstanding feat just to keep the air traffic moving in the midst of what so easily could have been chaos. Besides the test flights there were aircraft arriving to be processed, others were departing after receiving their clearance, as well as many other visitors on transport flights or liaison duties and, amazingly, arrivals on cross-country training flights.

Because of the urgency aircraft would be given clearance to take off even though other aircraft would be on the approach to land. The duration of test flights had to be kept to a minimum although conducting the same thorough examination. An illustration of this came when one test pilot was lined up for take-off in a P-51 while the B-24 ahead had just climbed to about 200 feet, retracted the undercarriage before then turning into the circuit lowering the wheels for landing as he did so. Thinking that the B-24 pilot had a problem there was concern, but back came the reply, 'No problem, it flies, everything works and time's a-wastin'. On many occasions crew chiefs had to fly as co-pilots on B-24s to enable as many aircraft as possible to be checked out.

Because of the intensity of the flying programme during the invasion month the possibility of an accident loomed large, but it was the unexpected that would make it a sad period. On 12 June 1944 a crew chief taxiing a newly arrived B-17 across the main runway thought he saw another aircraft about to land. He stood hard on the brakes forcing the aircraft to stand on its nose which completely crumpled back to the cockpit windscreen. There was no aircraft landing and it was assumed that the engineer had seen a bird out of the corner of his eye. Whatever the reason the Fortress would be staying at Warton for a much longer time than scheduled.

It was also on the 12th that the first of two fatal accidents occurred as a new P-51D shed a wing during a routine test flight with the aircraft crashing into the opposite bank of the River Ribble which runs past the airfield. The wreckage was recovered and placed into a corner of Hangar No.6 for detailed examination. As the aircraft was flying straight and level at the time of the accident the wing detachment was a cause for concern. The following day two P-51Ds flown by Warton test pilots were put through full aerobatic routines without any problems and the crash was assumed to be an isolated incident. On 17 June 1944 a newly arrived Mosquito P.R.XVI was test flown but belly-landed upon its return to Warton after a systems failure, leaving the sleek machine with its nose buried in a hedge before the runway threshold. Just ten days after the Mosquito incident disaster struck once again as another P-51D Mustang was involved in a fatal accident which was a carbon copy of the one on the 12th. The aircraft was at about 7,000ft to the north of the airfield, flying in a clear blue sky, when the starboard wing detached from the aeroplane which then dived into the ground. It was reported that the pilot could have baled out, but kept applying power at intervals to try to steer the machine away from houses. Once again the wreckage was carefully investigated and, although it was consistent with the first crash, there were no obvious clues as to the precise nature of the structural failure. A space was cleared in Hangar No.5 for a new P-51D to be placed on jacks for undercarriage tests to be undertaken, for it was that area which was under suspicion. It had been discovered that the right undercarriage leg had dropped during flight and had completely twisted around. Extensive tests revealed that after a number of changes in the P-51D model, wing-root fatigue was the cause of the problem. The changes in the later type included the addition of an extra machine-gun in each wing, as well as a number of other features, putting greater stresses on the wing than the earlier P-51B and C models. Presumably as a weight saving measure, the undercarriage uplocks on the earlier Mustangs had been omitted from the P-51D allowing the wheel legs to bounce around in their wells with only hydraulic pressure to hold them when the undercarriage was selected up. Any surge or fall in pressure would allow them to force the wheel doors open in flight, extending the wheels and, at a reasonable speed, ripping the wing off. The bouncing around had caused the fatigue and the resulting structural failure. The Warton findings were quickly transmitted to the manufacturers and to USAAF Headquarters, with the result that P-51B type uplocks were retrofitted to all D models and the modification fitted to all new aircraft coming from the North American Aviation production lines. The expertise of the BAD.2 engineers had unravelled the mystery but had paid a high price with the loss of two test pilots.

If the problem had not been solved it would, no doubt, have cost many more lives. It was to the great credit of all concerned that the Warton air traffic continued to move at a high rate, because during June US Army's Engineering Aviation Battalion had arrived at BAD.2 to renew the perimeter track which had badly deteriorated through the sheer volume of aircraft using it. The original design of the airfield was as an RAF fighter station and the taxi-track had remained the same even though the runways had been lengthened and strengthened. The weight of numerous B-24s and B-17s trundling over it had made the track progressively worse

After a difficult month one highlight was the appearance on 28 June 1944 of the new P-61 Black Widow night fighter. The fighter landed at Warton only two days after its existence had been officially announced by the US War Department. Naturally, there was considerable interest in the aircraft not only from the flying personnel but from the air-minded ground crews too.

After the earlier departure of the station's anti-aircraft guns the base seemed vulnerable to air attack, but as the Luftwaffe's long-range raids had dwindled it was unlikely that BAD.2 would be targeted. It was a mystery why the Germans never bombed Burtonwood or Warton, as one large attack on each would have caused complications for the air offensive, especially with so many aircraft parked on both airfields.

The Aircraft Salvage Department usually had a straightforward job of taking the damaged aircraft apart to preserve the good spares and saving the taxpayers a great deal of money. Occasionally the task was made difficult and sometimes dangerous, as demonstrated one day when the section was relieving a B-24 of its top turret when a high-explosive cannon shell with detonator intact was lodged in the turret frame. One C-47 arrived to be scrapped but it was found that a box stowed in the rear fuselage contained German land mines and twenty rifles. The Ordnance Department was quickly on the scene to remove the box and, once disabled, they probably made excellent souvenirs, as they were never seen again.

The urgent need for P-51s reached its peak in July 1944 when there were a great many on the airfield. After clearance, they required ferrying, with the pilots of the 310th Ferrying Squadron working overtime. The ramp near the control tower had two lines of Mustangs running the entire length with others dispersed around the base waiting to go through Hangar No.5. The tower ramp was also used for visiting aircraft and one afternoon a pilot from a fighter base returned to where he had parked his Mustang to find that the super efficient engineers of BAD.2 had taken it into Hangar No.5 and were already working on it!

Information arrived at Warton which cheered the troops as it told that two of the P-51s bought in the War Bond Drive had been successful in action. The *Mazie R* had destroyed an Me 109 while serving with the 357th Fighter Group and *Pride of the Yanks* had destroyed two enemy aircraft while on a mission to Leipzig. The Mustang named *Too Bad*, as a tribute to BAD .2, had yet to score.

The morning of 23 August 1944 was like any other day at Warton with numerous aircraft movements and with the work continuing at a steady pace, although at a little less hectic rate than the two previous months. The weather was fine with some broken cloud but with the prospect of rain showers later in the morning. As this was not unusual for the Lancashire coast area there was no real concern among the air crews. Just after 1030 hours Warton's control tower received a priority radio call from Burtonwood advising that a severe electrical storm was heading in the direction of Warton and to request that any aircraft in flight should return to the airfield as soon as possible. Two B-24 Liberators were on test flights from BAD.2 with both immediately setting course for base but for one of them it was too late. The skies darkened while the aircraft was on the approach, with the storm breaking over Warton as the B-24 arrived. The pilot attempted to overshoot and radioed that his instruments were not reading but he would climb away from the airfield. Unfortunately, nothing was heard from him again as the Liberator had crashed into the Holy Trinity School in the centre of Freckleton village, completely demolishing the building before slewing across a main road destroying a small car used by servicemen from the station. This horrific accident cost the lives of sixty-one, with thirty-eight of those killed being young children. The storm which passed up the west coast was one of the worst ever seen in the area, ripping off roofs, knocking down walls and destroying crops, but all of that damage paled into insignificance compared with the loss of life from the crash of the bomber. The second Liberator had cleared the area as the storm had hit Warton, the crew being unaware of the accident until after they had landed.

Every man at Warton was affected by the Freckleton crash, but the disaster could not be allowed to affect the station's performance and it was fortunate that Bing Crosby and other entertainers arrived soon afterwards, with this serving to alleviate some of the sadness which prevailed at the base. During the course of the year many entertainers had visited Warton, including Glenn Miller and his Orchestra as well as a number of film stars. However, the Crosby visit was most timely in the wake of the accident.

Early in September the first of the new A-26 Invader medium bombers arrived at BAD.2. This type would start to replace the popular A-20 Havoc. In the specialized system Hangar No.3 handled B-24s, C-47s and the occasional B-17, while Hangar No.4 had converted from B-17s to B-24s. In addition to the overhauls, a number of B-24s were converted to a variety of duties, including those for 'Carpetbagger' operations (the code-name for clandestine duties), while others had large fuel tanks fitted into the fuselage to carry much needed fuel to the continent. Hangar No.4 also coped with an urgent influx of C-47s for engine changes and a period when P-47 Thunderbolts needed wing brackets and the installation of water injection systems.

Hangar No.5 handled the P-51 line. The first P-51Bs arriving in England had passed through to have an additional eighty-five gallon fuel tank installed in the fuselage. Wing mountings were also fitted to enable the aircraft to carry drop tanks. Another task was the fitting of G-suit adapters for the Mustang pilots. After the invasion, Hangar No.5 also handled the P-47s urgently needed for the fighter-bomber role supporting the ground forces fighting on the continent. Hangars No.6 and 7 belonged to Flight Test where aircraft were prepared for flight, being cleared by the BAD.2 test pilots before being delivered to their operational units. Hangars No.1 and 2 handled a variety of types, including the liaison aeroplanes. Hangars No.31 and 32 were located on the far side of the airfield across from the seven main hangars and adjacent to the River Ribble. Completed in the autumn of 1944, their main programme did not commence until later in the war when they were used for the assembly of Waco CG-4 and CG-15 gliders, which would be used in the assault during the crossing of the Rhine. Other hangars situated at Warton were used for a variety of work or storage tasks.

Although there were not enough fully trained technicians to staff every hangar, crews were streamlined and spread throughout the facility. Production progressed so rapidly that any backlog soon disappeared. Teams were becoming so efficient that they were beginning to run out of work, especially as the 8th Bomber Command made a decision to limit the number of heavy bombers on the airfield at any one time to twenty-five. However, a programme which showed that at least fifteen bombers could be handled by Warton every single day was submitted to Bomber Command and the number restriction was soon lifted.

The progressive build-up of men and material on the Continent meant an even greater need for air transport, with orders being received by the 87th Air Transport Squadron for a move to AAF Station 519 at Grove in Berkshire, which had to be completed by 18 September 1944.

Straightforward maintenance and overhaul work was continuing steadily, although the number of aircraft arriving for modifications had increased. Some P-51 Mustangs were to be converted to the F-6 photographic reconnaissance version, while B-24 Liberators were returning for modification into weather reconnaissance, night leaflet dropping and additional aircraft for the fuel carrying role. Two B-17s had arrived during September for conversion into weather reconnaissance aircraft and fifty 'kits' for the assembly of Piper L-4 Grasshopper liaison aircraft had been transported by road to Warton.

Besides the scheduled tasks, many unofficial modifications were carried out at the request of various units. One such came from Troop Carrier Command (TCC) as the C-47 pilots had complained about the lack of protection from small arms fire while on low-level parachute drops. Warton's Aircraft Salvage Department rose to the challenge by arranging for armour-plated sections removed from scrapped B-24s to be cut down and shaped as back and foot plates for installation into the C-47s. It came as a great pleasure to all sections when BAD.2 received a memo from TCC Headquarters expressing their thanks as the modification had saved the lives of the two pilots of a C-47 after the cockpit had been riddled by machine-gun fire. It also reported another incident which took place as a C-47 was taking off with two CG-4 gliders in tow when the transport's undercarriage collapsed. As the port propeller hit the concrete runway a large piece of blade broke off and sliced through the nose of the C-47 striking the pilot's seat before smashing the arm of the co-pilot's chair. Undoubtably the armour plate had saved both pilots as it was noted that a similar incident before the fitting of the armour plate had cost the life of a pilot while his co-pilot had lost a leg.

Following the move of the 87th ATS to Grove, the 312th Ferrying Squadron had arrived at Warton from BAD.3 at Langford Lodge but, before they had chance to settle in, they too were transferred to Grove on 27 September 1944.

On 5 October 1944 an amazing series of incidents brought Warton to a stand-still as three aircraft came to grief within fifteen minutes of each other. The runway 15/33, which was 3,960 feet long, was seldom used for operations and normally acted as a parking area for the overflow of aircraft. However, on that particular day the wind was extremely strong bringing the runway into use. Aeroplanes were approaching over the River Ribble to land in a north-north-westerly direction. There was a slight depression where it intersected the main runway which meant many aircraft became airborne again after touching down and an unsuspecting pilot would suddenly have his hands full trying to get the aeroplane down again before he ran out of runway. The first aircraft to be involved was a B-24 from the 466th Bomb Group at Attlebridge in Norfolk which after the intersection became airborne again and, after touching down for a second time, ran off the end of the runway and into the soft grass, ripping off the nose wheel leg. As Warton was its usual busy self, an incident like this could not be allowed to stop flight operations but, just twelve minutes later, an A-20 arrived and although the pilot had been warned of the problem, the same thing happened! This time the Havoc pilot had not only to stop but steer his aircraft around the Liberator which was sitting tail high in the grass. Through a large slice of luck he was able to veer off the runway onto the grass missing the B-24 completely. Despite the two machines in the grass at the end of the runway and not too far from Hangar No.7, it was thought to be safe to let a P-51 land on arrival from Speke. Once again the aircraft became airborne after passing the depression with the Mustang leaping into the air before dropping back onto the runway and racing towards the two crashed bombers. With much power being applied, the Merlin's torque pulled the brand-new P-51 off the runway and onto the grass where it ground-looped. The pilot was able to climb out and was soon on his way to hospital to join the bomber crews for a check-up. Luckily there were no injuries but only three bent aeroplanes and a lot of dented pride. It was later concluded that the runway depression, the strong gusting wind and the pilots' unfamiliarity with the airfield had conspired to cause the accidents.

On 7 October a number of men were transferred from the Maintenance Division on temporary assignment to Grove to assemble L-4 Grasshoppers, as no room was available at any of the air depots at that time. One week later the 310th Ferrying Squadron, which was classed as 'Warton's own', was also transferred to Grove, although seventy-five pilots were left behind and assigned to the Flight Test Department of BAD.2. Those who stayed would have a similar role in the delivery of aircraft as machines were, in some cases, delivered to airfields on the Continent, while some of the more experienced were trained as test pilots.

The ingenuity of Warton's engineers in devising methods to improve efficiency was endless, with working times being reduced on every type of aircraft. One example was a tool invented to ease the inspection of engine magnetos on the Mustangs as the design enabled mechanics to remove the rear casing screws without having to remove the complete magneto from the engine, thereby saving two hours per magneto or four hours per aircraft. The original method was difficult, time-consuming and also produced many skinned knuckles for the mechanics.

In the Engine Repair Department the last Allison engine for the P-38 Lightning was tested on 9 October 1944, with this being the 2,586th of its type to go through BAD.2. When the facility was established the engine test stands were able to run both Allison and Merlins. Initially, trouble was encountered as the engines ran too cool and two bypass valves were devised which not only solved the problem but also decreased time on the whole test procedure. The great requirement for engines saw the section expand into Hangar No.14 which had been used by the Salvage Department. This move allowed better facilities for engine dismantling and clearing, with the production lines being rearranged to operate more efficiently and a later expansion saw the engine section take over Hangar No.15, formerly the home of the Dispatch Department. The end of the Allison production meant that all efforts could be concentrated on the increasing demand for Merlins for fitment, or as spare engines for the P-51 units of the 8th and 9th Air Forces.

In the Bombsight Department a directive had been received expressing concern about the stabilising mount of the Norden B-7 bombsight, with Warton's technicians finding a solution by modifying a template designed by the manufacturers. The Norden section of the department also constructed a C-1 autopilot mock-up which enabled line crews at their bases to complete on-the-spot troubleshooting by publishing instructions for engaging and adjusting autopilots during air tests.

The 56th Field Hospital had been attached to the BAD.2 station hospital but, on 28 October, the airfield had to accommodate forty-six visiting C-47s which had arrived to transfer the whole of the 56th to Le Bouscat, France. The operation ran smoothly with Warton's highly experienced air traffic controllers co-ordinating the movement with normal ferrying and flight tests.

In November 1944 a war-weary C-47 by the name of *Chukky* arrived at Warton for scrapping after being declared surplus by Troop Carrier Command. However, to the BAD.2 engineers the aircraft seemed too good to go to the salvage section so, as with the P-51 *Spare Parts*, permission was requested for the aeroplane to be rebuilt for station use. The olive-drab painted machine was completely stripped down, worn-out parts replaced and a number of additions were incorporated to make the aircraft 'that little bit special'. The now gleaming C-47 was rolled out of Hangar 4 and given the name *Jackpot* in honour of the Head of the Maintenance Department who, in 1941, had been one of the pilots responsible for introducing the C-47 type into military service. The aircraft served Warton well after flying many morale boosting 'supply' missions to the continent for items in short supply in Britain. The Hangar No.4 people must have done a great job because this aircraft flew for many years after the war while operating on the French civil register and was last heard of in storage near Paris in 1971.

On 29 November BAD.2 had the first serious aircraft accident since the crash of the B-24 at Freckleton just three months earlier. Two of the new A-26 Invaders collided after take-off for delivery to the 409th Bomb Group of the 9th Bomber Command, based at Bretigny in France. The first four A-26s to be cleared by Warton had been delivered in September with these being followed by eight in October but, by November, the BAD.2 engineers involved in the aircraft's processing had gone into top gear as 115 Invaders were completed and readied for delivery. The first of the type to arrive at Warton were A-26Bs, with a vast array of armament causing much surprise among the aviators and ground crews as the aircraft's nose contained six machine guns, while remotely controlled dorsal and ventral turrets each carried two machine guns. This standard armament was supplemented by eight more guns in packs under the wings and, with all of these guns being the heavy fifty-calibre type, the A-26 had more than twice the firepower of a P-47 Thunderbolt plus a bomb load of up to 4,000lb, making the Invader a potent aeroplane. There was also a provision for replacing the nose guns with a seventy-five millimetre cannon, but no such modification was carried out at BAD.2. The A-26 was a new aircraft with which the Warton technicians had to quickly acquaint themselves and it was generally well accepted, although it was prone to nose-wheel collapse. The two A-26s involved in the collision had been collected by pilots of the 409th Bomb Group, with the accident happening just after take-off as the aircraft circled the airfield. Both machines fell into the River Ribble estuary and, despite the best efforts of the Lytham lifeboat and small boats from the base, the airmen had died on impact. One of the aircraft, which lies in the mud where it fell, can still be seen to this day and brave attempts by aviation archaeologists to remove it are always frustrated by the tide which quickly covers the area when recovery is underway.

In the production records of BAD.2 there is no mention of the C-109 Liberator tankers and USAAF records show that this type was only used for carrying fuel to advanced bases in China to support the B-29 Superfortress units operating against Japan. Although the Liberator fuel-carrying version was designated C-109, the conversions carried out at BAD.2 were not classed as such but remained B-24s. Four bombardment groups from the 2nd Air Division had some of their aircraft converted to tankers and were given the task of hauling fuel and supplies to General Patton's Third Army and the Twelfth Army Group, fighting on the Continent. Although the fitting of fuel tanks to the B-24s was also carried out at other air depots, the bulk of the work was allocated to Warton.

As production increased during 1943 hangar personnel had worked eight hour shifts but, from February 1944, twelve hour duties were introduced with work equally rotated, continuing around the clock. The stress of this working with only occasional time off was beginning to tell on the health of some of the men and in May 1944, after medical advice, the working schedule was revised to allow all personnel to have one day off per week. It would be the following October before the shift system returned to eight hour working although, through an efficiency drive, there was little reduction in the output of aircraft.

Although titled the Bombsight Department, this section also completed work on autopilot systems in almost equal proportions. In November 1944 the department accomplished the installation of the newly arrived C-1 electronic autopilot into a C-47 transport. The wiring and installation plans were devised by the engineers of the section as this work on the aircraft type had never been carried out. The old A-3 autopilot was removed and the new C-1 installed with the aeroplane being flight tested in less than one week. Reports on the success were sent to the Douglas Aircraft Corporation with the C-1 being recommended as a more efficient alternative as a result of BAD.2's trials.

The departure of the ferry squadron had left a handsome terminal building vacant and this was quickly taken over as headquarters of the Flight Test Department. With the extra space a Pilot's Transition Training School was established for the purpose of training and checking out all pilots on every type of American aircraft to be flown into Britain. An Aircraft Delivery section was also established to take over some of the task of the ferry squadrons and this department was soon at work as a number of new B-24s had to be delivered to the 15th Air Force in Italy.

New modifications of aircraft types became a standard part of BAD.2's working programme for, besides the demands of the 'Carpetbagger' project, other B-24 rôles included the night leaflet aircraft and the requirement for a flare dropping machine code-named 'Firefly Big'. A similar project was added when A-20 Havocs were converted as 'Firefly Little'. Another request received from the combat units was for A-26 Invaders to be fitted with three signal lights on each wingtip and once again the Warton technicians had to design and install a system to meet the requirement. A strange request came from AFSC Headquarters for flak repair kits to be manufactured as the linemen in combat groups were spending too much of their time making them. The BAD.2 people devised a system to make the patches in six different sizes and proceeded to produce them at a rate of 10,000 per day!

On 15 December 1944 a ceremony was held at the doors of Hangar No.4 as its 1,000th B-24 was rolled out with the record showing that ninety-two men had worked on the aircraft during its process of modification and inspection.

As the war on the Continent intensified the requirement for light liaison aircraft increased and assembly of kit form machines saw engineers from Warton's Engine Repair Department being allocated to work on L-4 Grasshopper and L-5 Sentinal types with effect from 16 December. The facilities at Hangar No.15 were made available for the task, with the personnel of the Despatch Department having to relocate to Hangar No.13 in the space formerly occupied by the Allison engine assembly line. This extra production of liaison types commenced on 18 December with the first aircraft, an L-5B, being test flown just two days later.

The Aircraft Accident Board investigating the crash of the B-24 in Freckleton issued their report on the accident which included a number of recommendations concerning the senior officers of BAD.2. The base would have to appoint an aviator in the full capacity of Operations Officer while a Flying Control Officer was to be a ground officer, having graduated from the Flying Control School, and would perform only those duties for which he was trained. Warton felt strongly that these recommendations reflected badly on those officers carrying out those duties at the time of the crash as their actions could have had no bearing on the outcome.

Cause for concern came through a report which informed BAD.2 that a number of hard-line German prisoners located in a mill at nearby Kirkham were flying personnel and, in the event of a breakout, immediate action should be taken to prevent them getting on to the base in a possible attempt to steal aircraft to make good their escape. The concern was increased on Christmas Eve when it was discovered that 28,000 prisoners within a thirty-miles radius of Preston were planning a mass escape with the intention of sabotaging as many military installations as possible. Warton was put on full alert with personnel being armed and British troops being available to assist if required. Three days later the emergency was scaled down, although held in abeyance for immediate reintroduction if necessary. It should be noted that there were 838 aircraft on the base at that time!

The incredible facts and figures required to operate BAD.2 came in a report issued at the end of 1944 which saw the Supply Division having received 50,000 tons of supplies and shipped approximately 45,000 tons of completed items. An average of 293 trucks were dispatched weekly, hauling material to all parts of Britain, while 140 railway wagons were incoming, and 123 were sent out. During the year 302,482 items of varying quantities were requested and 61,000 teletypes received.

The year 1945 dawned with a request from the Liberator groups for replacement seats for the pilots of their B-24s. The aircraft were originally fitted with armoured seats for the two pilots. While these afforded excellent protection from flak fragments the seats were cumbersome, restricting movement and, in the case of emergency, a quick exit from the aircraft. Known as 'coffin seats' to the B-24 crews, Warton had started replacing these seats a few months earlier but as new machines arrived from the manufacturers with improved seats, the replacement programme came to an end. However, the new request started the work once more and external armour was fitted to the fuselage sides under the cockpit windows of the B-24s, much to the relief of the Liberator pilots.

An interesting task was also started in January when work commenced on eight P-38 Lightnings arrived from AAF Station 237 at Greencastle in Northern Ireland. That station, which was a satellite of BAD.3 at Langford Lodge, had classed the aircraft as war-weary, sending them to BAD.2 for disposal. After inspection the Warton engineers felt that there was airframe-life still remaining in the aeroplanes and initiated 1,000 hour inspections, overhaul and stage modifications not previously incorporated in the P-38s. The war-weary status was then removed with all of the aircraft being ferried to units of the 9th Air Force. Another job undertaken by Warton was to commence the removal of engines from P-51s with over 200 hours in service and fitting new engines, as signs of wear had been detected in the 100 hour inspections.

On 22 January 1945 BAD.2 received a communication requiring the transfer of personnel to the infantry because of the heavy losses sustained during the fighting on the continent. Warton detailed thirty-three men from the Administration Division but, before the order could be issued, another directive arrived stating that the BAD.2 quota would now be 395. The unfortunate airmen had to be fully equipped and ready to leave by 30 January. The war situation was obviously acute as it was stated that even prisoners could be released from the Guard House. The teletype produced an even greater shock on 12 February when it stated that a further 450 men were needed, with regular Air Force men being exempted unless they wished to volunteer, needless to say, there were no takers amongst the latter.

The post-war potential of Warton was already being studied and this was revealed when a delegation arrived from Washington on 17 February to inspect the base. The station was deemed to be ideal as a school for all branches of vocational training for civilian life with an estimated 8,000 troops able to receive training.

During February one of the more noteworthy projects for BAD.2 was the contribution by the personnel of their chocolate and cigarette rations to Russian servicemen who had been working as forced labour for the Germans but who had been freed by the Allied advance in Europe. A large number of the Russians were in a camp at Worthing in Sussex and, as it was going to be some time before they were returned to their homeland, the Americans felt that they could receive some comforts while they were in England. On 22 February a C-47, named Bear Hug for the occasion, was flown down to the airfield at Ford carrying a load of supplies for the Soviets. A few days later Warton received a warm letter of thanks from the leader of the ex-prisoners with a copy being given to everyone at BAD.2 for their contribution.

During February the transfer of a further 106 men to the ground forces in Europe caused problems in a number of sections as the shortage forced a change in shifts which almost eliminated night working. The problem was compounded when it was learned that BAD.2 would be receiving a large number of gliders for assembly with 1,600 being scheduled for delivery in the following two months. The gliders would each be packed into five boxes which meant that the base would have to handle a total of 8,000 packing cases. Because of the release of troops to the infantry it soon became obvious that Warton could not handle the extra task and a detachment of men from BAD.1, who had experience in the assembly of gliders, were assigned to BAD.2. As the gliders arrived they were uncrated with the boxes being broken down and the timber stored for other uses. The assembly of the Waco CG-4A gliders commenced on 22 February 1945.

Other engineering programmes which commenced during February were the equipping of propeller anti-icing systems to all B-24 Liberators due to return to American in a project known as 'Back to the States', as no aircraft would be allowed to depart without the system being fitted. Ten B-24s had arrived during February for this work to start. Another project was the manufacture of new forward entrance doors for B-17s, but the shortage of hinges arriving from the manufacturers in the United States was slowing down work. As the doors were urgently needed by the combat groups it was decided that BAD.2 would produce the hinges locally by casting and milling them to a finish. The programme was greatly speeded up by the local production as the door situation required a priority status.

The Ordnance Branch devised a method for producing the T-3 chaff bomb with this arrangement including the splitting of a 100lb bomb into two pieces just above the fins and then inserting a wooden frame to hold the chaff, before removing and modifying the nose of the weapon to carry a timer and charge. The bomb proved to be highly successful and the design was adopted by the USAAF as it fully met their requirements.

The AFSC had reported to the United States that the 8th Bomber Command had requested to have the ball turrets of B-24s removed from all aircraft and felt that it was unnecessary to install such turrets into aircraft under manufacture. This suggestion was duly adopted and new B-24Ms began to arrive at Warton minus these turrets. Twenty-two of this version were assigned to the 15th Air Force operating in the Mediterranean Theatre of Operations (MTO) and were duly processed with the modification required for that area of operations. Amazingly, the 15th Air Force then called for ball turrets to be installed into these aircraft, with BAD.2 having to seek out as many turrets as possible from the scrap-man to be made serviceable and ready for fitment. This placed a great strain on the base as the work on the B-24s was already completed and the turret installation meant that the aircraft would have to re-join the production line bringing extra problems to the overworked engineers. As usual, the Warton planners came up with a revised schedule which saw sixteen of the B-24Ms completed in six days after the start on 15 February. With other Liberators already programmed for work the turret fitment produced a shortage of hangar space, but the work was completed.

The US 9th Bomber Command was concerned about the A-26 Invader's bombing system, which had shown itself to be vulnerable to dampness during winter operations from bases in France. A more rigid inspection of the affected parts was instituted and experiments on improvements and remedies were carried out. The new B-24Ms were also fitted with the same all-electric A-4 bombing system as the Invaders so it was anticipated that similar trouble could arise with the Liberators and steps were taken to solve the problem before it arose.

The personnel of the 310th Ferrying Squadron who were on detached service with the Maintenance Division were relieved of their assignment during February and returned to their parent unit, the 31st Air Transport Group of the 302nd Air Transport Wing. The Ferrying Squadron had been transferred in November 1944 to the 31st ATG from the 27th ATG, who were based at AAF Station 519 at Grove. As the 310th FS detachment was transferred the Maintenance Division was relieved of the task of ferrying aircraft and the Flight Test Department reverted to its original role.

In March the Supply Division received fewer than expected glider crates, as only 1,270 arrived, which was enough to complete 254 aircraft. The majority of these were the well-known CG-4A type, but a few were the later CG-15s and the glider situation escalated as the total number of boxes received was 2,000, enough for 400 aeroplanes. As a number of gliders were completed word was received that another 800 crates had arrived in Liverpool and were awaiting transport to Warton.

The Armament Department's work schedules began to increase dramatically but, with the loss of many of its personnel to the infantry, this put a great strain onto the section. Additional work included the harmonization of gun sight cameras on the P-51 Mustangs and this was the first time the task had been allocated to BAD No.2. Completed aircraft were delivered to combat units with this work carried out and also now having a full load of ammunition. The increasing output of A-26 Invaders put a further load on the Armament Department as it had been requested that the underwing gun packs for this type should now start to be fitted. The C-47s arriving at Warton for a complete overhaul were in an extremely poor state with many of them having flown over 2,000 hours. The aircraft had been in constant use in all conditions of service with little time for inspection or maintenance and the work was allocated to Hangar No.4. The work included engine changes, fuel tanks being replaced, electrical systems being updated, new autopilots being installed, blind landing equipment being fitted and a complete set of de-icer boots being fitted for each aircraft. A great amount of metal work was required which was mainly due to battle damage, but repairs to doors and new floors had to be fitted. The undercarriages were removed and cleaned, as many were clogged up with mud and stones from operations off forward airfields on the Continent. Parts had to be manufactured in a number of cases and after a new paint-job the whole programme was a credit to BAD.2 with the 302nd Air Transport Wing expressing their great satisfaction with both the operation and appearance of the C-47s when they were returned to the Wing.

On 20 March 1945 a surprise visit by the Inspector General in the 8th Air Force's only B-25 Mitchell caught BAD.2 off guard but the general was pleased with what he saw and an encouraging report on the visit was issued. Following on from that visit a Beech C-45 arrived bringing five senior officers from the USAAF's Air Inspector's Section and, after a thorough inspection, they departed having been satisfied with everything they had seen.

A public relations exercise took place on 23 March when the Mayor of Preston was invited to christen a new P-51D with the name of *Winged Victory*. The ceremony was to provide publicity for the film of that name showing that week in both Preston and Blackpool with the proceeds going to RAF and USAAF charities.

The glider programme had been suspended but was resumed in April, although the shortage of men to disassemble the crates required the base to take advantage of an offer of Spanish prisoners of war to take on general labouring duties and 100 were made available to the Supplies Division to help alleviate the situation.

Also during April, a number of visits were paid to Warton by members of the British Air Ministry to survey the airfield as a possible post-war municipal airport for nearby Preston.

In the Engine Repair Department the month of April had been a significant one for the Packard Merlin production line. With much activity the section saw the 2,500th engine successfully overhauled, tested and dispatched to a combat unit or used as a replacement power plant for some of the P-51s. It was noteworthy that the high rate of production attained was due to an efficiency drive which succeeded in almost halving the 500 hour period originally allocated for each engine. Morale boosting figures arriving from the United States reported that the BAD.2 engine unit had achieved the greatest production figures, easily beating those of other air depots.

Early in May, information was received that forty C-47s would be arriving at Warton for engine changes and this programme had to be given priority status over the B-24 redeployment project, with three hangars being made available. BADA Headquarters requested that the aircraft be made available for delivery by 22 May 1945, but the Maintenance Department had already scheduled the deadline for two days earlier.

On 7 May 1945 unofficial reports announced the defeat of Germany. It was later announced that Prime Minister Winston Churchill would call Victory in Europe (VE) Day at 1500 hours on the following day and King George VI would speak to the nation at 2100 hours. It was also decreed that 8 and 9 May 1945 would be set aside as national holidays for the celebration of victory.

After a short break to enjoy the festivities the work in progress continued with the order to replace the C-47 engines still in place but by the middle of May none of these aircraft had arrived at Warton.

The man-hour reduction on the B-24 programme was not implemented and work continued on the Liberators at the normal rate until the C-47s appeared. To add to the work scheduling, word was received that a further fifty-nine B-24s would be arriving from Stansted, as well as fifty-three others from Langford Lodge and one from Burtonwood. The order also stated that these aircraft would be joining the redeployment programme and it was required that twelve machines per day would have to be delivered commencing on the 23rd of that month.

The ending of the war against Germany seemed to have little effect on the work programme, although the first personnel to be going home were notified, with arrangements being made for their transportation to the United States. On 18 May all personnel were directed to see the movie *Two Down and One to Go* which included details on the defeat of Germany and Italy but stressed the task ahead in achieving a similar victory over the ruthless Japanese. Far from boosting morale as intended, it made some of the men think they would being heading to the Pacific to continue the fight.

On the last day of May the 2213th Truck Company (Aviation) departed BAD.2 for AAF Station 547 at Abbots Ripton, Huntingdonshire. The unit had served Warton from the early days but it would be the first of many such movements.

By the end of the month 120 B-24s had arrived for the redeployment project and the engine change C-47s had eventually started to appear. Also during May, fifty-one P-51 Mustangs had been processed and delivered but, this time, it was not to combat units but to Speke aerodrome at Liverpool for their return by sea to the United States.

The rundown of the various specialised areas commenced on 31 May, when orders were received from BADA Headquarters that the processing of spark plugs should end immediately and all other types of unnecessary work could be terminated. The glider project was officially ended with the order that all completed airframes and unbuilt sections should be disposed of and any personnel involved should be transferred to the B-24 project. Almost immediately after this order was received, the 9th Troop Carrier Command requested that all complete gliders should be made operational and ready for delivery, with 103 CG-4As and CG-15s being available for collection. Early in June a fleet of C-47s arrived at BAD.2 to tow away the gliders, much to the relief of Air Traffic Control and the Alert Crew who had had to operate normally although the gliders took up large areas of the airfield.

The work on autopilots, gunsights and bombsights was also run down and the order to pack them for return to America was received. The efficiency of the BAD.2 engineers surprised BADA Headquarters when it was found that at least four C-47s would be required to transport the packed equipment. It was a great pleasure when the bombsights left the base as a vault had been required for their storage with an around-the-clock guard in place. This boring duty would be no more.

During the month of June 1945 the redeployment of the Supplies Division saw large stocks of material being dispatched to the USAAF in Germany, with many other items being packed for shipping to the United States. The glider packing cases provided the wood but other items, including greaseproof paper and nails, started to run out and urgent requests were sent to other units for supplies. Besides the American shipments, almost 1,000 crates of components were transferred to the RAF to support the US types of aircraft being operated by the British. Despite the loss of personnel through demobilisation and transfers, the work continued smoothly, with a large roller conveyor system being set up to accelerate the packing and stencilling time.

Twenty-two B-24 Liberators, which had sought refuge in neutral Sweden during operations over Germany, would be made flyable and returned to Warton for a complete overhaul and were then to be added to the redeployment programme. The aircraft started to arrive in the first few days of June and were duly processed with the others. By the middle of that month 133 B-24s had been delivered, with a further fifty-seven undergoing flight tests. Crews of Air Transport Command had been detailed to ferry the bombers out at a rate of at least five per day but this was exceeded on most days. In addition to the B-24 project, it was found that a single Liberator was serving at the Aircraft and Armament Experimental Establishment (A&AEE) at Boscombe Down in Wiltshire, with this aircraft having to be returned from the RAF to join the redeployment scheme.

The steady reduction in the number of personnel throughout the base had spread across most sections, which meant that those remaining would have to work just that much harder to meet deadlines which were still being set. One such deadline came for the Electrical Section as units operating A-26 Invaders were reporting serious problems with the wing flap gear-boxes and it was found that a large number of carbon pile voltage regulators would be required. As many of these had been crated up and shipped it was left to the electricians to recover regulators from those already scrapped but the job was completed by overhauling and modifying the various items. The Hydraulic Branch was also busy as an urgent requirement for wheels and brakes for A-26s had to be met.

The Engine Repair Department of the Maintenance Division had been engaged in engine testing since its establishment and it was on 20 June 1945 that last of 6,164 came off the assembly line. The Packard Merlin V-1650 was put through the usual test programme and ran perfectly but, instead on going into stock, it was decided that it would be a fitting end to the section if the engine went into service immediately. On the following morning it was duly installed in a P-51D, completed the ground engine runs and the aeroplane took to the air one day later. The engine figure quoted only accounts for the Allison and Merlin in-line engines and does not include the 126 radials which were completed before the airframe and engine specialization came into force.

The full redeployment schedule for the Maintenance Department was received from BADA Headquarters ordering a reduction in production of thirty-eight percent during June and July and fifty percent in August. With the programme well underway troops were arriving at Warton from every part of the ETO to be flown home. Each B-24 was able to carry ten passengers on makeshift seats in the bomb bay and other parts of the aircraft. The Liberators were still being flown by crews of the Air Transport Command.

On 22 June the Propeller Governor Section completed its last work on the Hamilton Standard and Curtiss Electric type airscrews. By the end of the month virtually every production line had come to an end and more than half of the Production Planning Section's manpower had been transferred or demobilised.

More senior officers arrived from London on 15 July to discuss the establishment of the Centralised Technical School No.1, which would retrain servicemen for trades after their return to civilian life. The title was later changed to the Warton American Technical School.

Despite the loss of large numbers of personnel the remaining staff at BAD.2 turned out 145 aircraft during July, with the last of the many, a C-47, being completed on the 27th of that month. However, it was 2 August 1945 when the last aircraft ever to be delivered from BAD.2, a B-24 Liberator, took off at 0900 hours amid great excitement and no small celebration of the occasion.

News of the Japanese surrender on 14 August 1945 reached Warton, with the news of the victory being greeted with great joy and a certain amount of relief for the men, who could possibly have been transferred to the Pacific once BAD.2 had finally ceased operations. There were a number of events to mark the end of the war, with celebration speeches, parties and, of course, religious services.

On Monday 20 August, over 2,000 people and the personnel from Warton crowded into Freckleton village for the dedication of a memorial playground in memory of those who died in the B-24 accident almost one year earlier. The playground and memorial stone were paid for by donations of the Warton troops and over 600 men from the base took an active part in its construction. Happily, the playground is still in use for its intended purpose today.

Four days later over 300 servicemen left Warton for Lytham station, to make the long train journey to Southampton for embarkation on the Queen Elizabeth for the voyage to New York and home. The troops were given a great send-off by the local people and Warton's own 523rd Army Air Force Band.

The end of August saw the official closure of Base Air Depot .2, with the release date of 1 September 1945 being noted in orders received from BADA Headquarters. Two days later the station was turned over to the new personnel arriving to staff the Warton American Technical School. All warehouses had been cleared out and these provided excellent classrooms for the Technical School, with the bulk of BAD.2's office equipment and supplies being passed to the new organisation.

The Technical School had the whole facility at its disposal to train for a variety of trades, with eighteen in all being available. Bulldozers and earth moving equipment roamed the airfield where the sleek P-51 Mustangs had been just weeks before. Beginner and refresher courses were offered, with building and electrical work being well catered for. However, the aeronautical engineering classes were popular, with an old B-17 and a B-24 to work on, as well as over forty different types of aero-engines to learn.

Classes commenced on 16 September 1945 with 4,000 servicemen taking advantage of each eight week term. However, on 11 January 1946 the last of the students departed and the school was closed, with its staff being transferred to a similar programme based in Germany to continue the trade-training for troops still serving on the continent. The school had been highly successful in training men for their return to civilian life as many had gone straight from their own education directly into the service. By the second week in February 1946 Warton had been completely vacated by the Americans and the station returned to its original owners, the Royal Air Force.

As the war drew to a close BAD.2 at Warton was given the title of 'The World's Greatest Air Depot'. When the production figures were released it was easy to see why, with 10,068 aircraft being processed, including 4,372 P-51 Mustangs and 2,894 B-24 Liberators, with a wide assortment of other American types making up the remainder. The total figure does not include the other 4,000 aircraft which passed through BAD No.2 for inspection only. During the depot's operational period over 45,000 aircraft movements were recorded, over 6,000 engines received complete overhauls and miscellaneous sections dealing with instruments, radios, guns, parachutes, life rafts, spark plugs and every other type of aviation material made more than two million items serviceable.

The title given to Warton was always disputed by BAD.1 at Burtonwood but Warton's production record could not be questioned and BAD.1 had to settle for 'The World's Largest Air Depot'! Whichever was the case, the 8th and 9th Air Forces could not have operated so efficiently without the skill and dedication of the men at the Base Air Depots.

The BAD.2 motto 'It can be done' was confirmed at the war's end, as its personnel ensured that 'It was done'. It is now over half a century since the Stars and Stripes were lowered for the last time at Warton. However, today the airfield is still at the forefront of world aviation, with BAE Systems employing some of the leading technicians and specialists. Nothing has changed!

One

The Early Days

GB 10 331 bc   **Warton**   Lfl. Kdo. 3   Januar 1943

Nur für den Dienstgebrauch!   Flugplatz   Karte 1:100000

Bild Nr. B.P.S. GB 7346   Länge (westl. Greenw.): 2° 52′ 30″   Nördl. Breite: 53° 44′ 30″   GB/E 8

v. 29. 9. 40   Zielhöhe über NN: 10 m

Flugplatz nach 2166 Z 10

v. 11. 2. 42   Maßstab: 1:25000

1. 3 Startbahnen, etwa 800 m, 800 m und 1300 m lang
2. Rollstraßen
Gleisanschluß nicht vorhanden.

This German reconnaissance photograph of Warton was dated 29 September 1940 when the area had been selected for the construction of a fighter airfield for the RAF. The airfield outline was inked in at a later date and issued to the Luftwaffe for information in January 1943. Surprisingly, the airfield was never attacked.

On 26 November 1942 Warton's ground staff were looking forward to the arrival of a flight of Lockheed P-38 Lightnings but, for one of them, things went wrong when the aircraft skidded off the main runway and into the rain-soaked grass. The rather mangled truck in the background was luckily unoccupied at the time the Lightning smashed into it. This aircraft, 43-2087, was a P-38F model taken over from a British contract but allocated a 1943 US serial number.

The Norden bombsight in this B-24D Liberator was completely covered, as per the regulations, as the instrument was rated as highly classified The armed guard security was relaxed later in the war when it became known that the Germans had full details of the bombsight.

Ending its career at Warton on 3 February 1943, this Bell P-39M Airacobra was a rare type in Britain. The serial number was 42-4833.

One of the first types into Warton was a Cessna UC-78 Bobcat which was used on communication duties. Although it was a pretty aeroplane, used widely by the USAAF, the Bobcat suffered some structural failures and was not popular with the ground crews. Warton's own UC-78 was 43-31827 named Bamboo Bomber.

Air Traffic Control was established with the help of the RAF using very basic equipment, which consisted of two Very pistols, one Aldis lamp and a radio. The incredible number of movements yet to come could never have been envisaged.

A Yank in the RAF! A Curtiss P-40B Tomahawk was used at Burtonwood as a communications aircraft by senior officers who were reluctant to part with the machine once their own UC-78 had arrived. The Tomahawk was a frequent visitor to Warton, usually on 'urgent' business.

In a colourful dedication ceremony the RAF handed Warton over to the USAAF on 17 July 1943. Outside the Flight Test hangars can be seen a shadow shaded B-17E, a UC-61 Forwarder, a P-39 Airacobra, an RAF Tiger Moth and the station's own B-26 Marauder *Demon Deacon*.

Photographed from the new American-style control tower, the hand-over parade reviewing officers salute as the Stars and Stripes is raised over Warton. The RAF band provided the musical accompaniment.

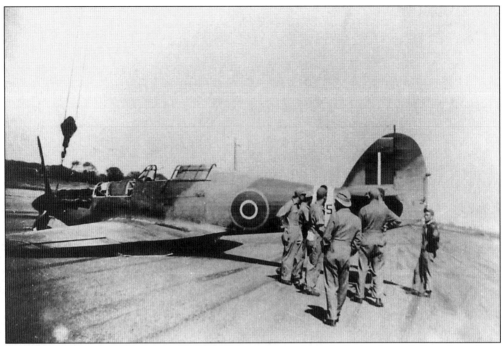

This RAF Hurricane added to the Warton repair quota after a belly-landing. A British working party arrived to restore the aeroplane and enjoy some fine American hospitality, perhaps taking longer than normal to do so!

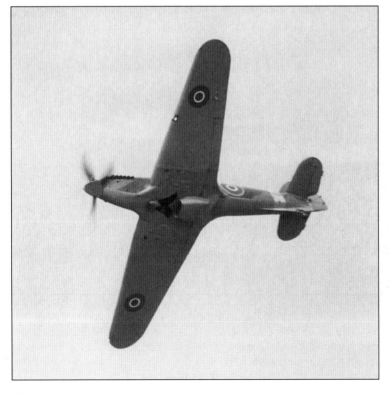

Duly repaired, the Hurricane put on a short flying display before returning to its own station.

An intriguing photograph of the ex-RAF Havoc AX924 flown by Fay Brandis of the 310th Ferry Squadron. The aircraft's original matt black colour scheme appears to have had olive drab shading applied, along with the US star insignia. Of more interest are the windows fitted along the rear cockpit decking.

The B-24H Liberator *Pregnant Peg*, number 42-7491 of the 392nd Bomb Group, force-landed at Ashill, Norfolk, on 30 October 1943. After several weeks repairing the aircraft a temporary airstrip was cleared and the Liberator was successfully flown out by Major Allen G. Russell of Ferry Command who had flown down from Warton to complete the operation. Sadly, the aircraft was lost on a mission to Oranienburg on 3 March 1944.

Looking west from the control tower towards Flight Test Hangars 6 and 7, a mixture of aircraft types include an Oxford and Dominie in US colours, while in the line-up is a Mustang in RAF markings. Newly arrived American P-51 Mustangs are parked along with P-38 Lightnings and P-47 Thunderbolts in November 1943.

In the opposite direction, the popularity of an American base with the RAF is evident, with a Beaufighter, a Hurricane, an Anson and a Tiger Moth seen with the American aircraft on Warton's hangar ramp.

Lieutenant Fay Brandis studies his blind flying results with the Link Trainer specialist Staff Sergeant, while other pilots wait their turn for instruction. Even the most experienced American pilots received extra training in blind flying techniques to cope with the British weather.

One of the harder jobs on a cold winter morning was the pulling through of the propellers which helped to circulate the oil in the engine cylinders.

The small patches show the extent of the repair after flak fragments had badly damaged this B-24. The aircraft had over 100 holes in the wings, rear fuselage and tail repaired and, of course, was completely resprayed before it left Warton.

Two
The Build Up

Lieutenant Burtie Orth poses the Piper L-4 Grasshopper liasion aircraft for Jack Knight's camera in January 1944. Orth was to lose his life in a P-51 Mustang a few months later.

A further example of a flak-damaged B-24, showing a large hole in the starboard wing and splinters in the engine nacelle. This aircraft arrived at BAD.2 on 9 February 1944 to add to the depot's normal work of inspection, overhaul and modification.

Major Charles Himes, BAD.2's chief test pilot, flies this P-47 Thunderbolt which had returned to Warton for overhaul. The aircraft, 42-8400, wears the code-letters of the 352nd Fighter Group and was the personal mount of ace Bill Whisner.

The winter of 1943-1944 was particularly hard for some of Warton's troops as 'Tent City' was to be their home until permanent accommodation was completed. Those from the 'sunshine states' found Lancashire's cold, damp weather and inevitable mud extremely demoralising.

Officers of the Flight Test department pose near *Short Fuse Sallee* which was the personal aircraft of Richard E. Turner, one of the top aces in the 354th Fighter Group. The aircraft had returned to BAD.2 for overhaul.

New P-51B Mustangs await test flights outside Hangar 6 on 25 February 1944. The nearest aircraft, 43-6562, joined the famous 4th Fighter Group but was shot down on 11 July 1944 with its pilot, Lt James S. Hanrahan being captured. He later escaped and returned to England.

When this line-up of mainly P-47 Thunderbolts was taken in March 1944 it had already been decreed that work on the heavy fighter would be allocated to BAD.1 at Burtonwood.

As personnel were arriving at Warton in large numbers the construction of the Nissen hut accommodation received urgent priority. Here the extension to Site 9 is well underway.

Warton's unique control tower was the only one of its type in Britain during the Second World War. The structure was dismantled in the early 1950s after the airfield had been purchased by the English Electric Company.

This photograph shows the extent of the work carried out on newly arrived aircraft by the BAD.2 engineers. Pictured in March 1944, the P-51B in Hangar 5 is undergoing complete inspection and installation of an eighty-five gallon fuel tank in the fuselage.

A number of Fortresses arrived at Warton for overhaul before returning to the United States as training aircraft. This B-17F was a veteran of over eighty missions while serving with the 306th Bomb Group.

The base hospital was considered to be one of the finest US military hospitals of its type in Britain, with over 100 beds available and equipped for every kind of medical emergency. In post-war years it continued in use as an RAF Medical Centre.

The main interest in this photograph is not the line-up of B-24s awaiting delivery, but on the right of the picture is the experimental B-17 named *The Dreamboat*. The aircraft was fitted out as a gunship, equipped with Liberator-type nose- and tail-gun turrets and other extra armament.

New B-24 Liberators processed at Warton were painted with the round insignia of the 2nd Air Division in preparation for their allocation to one of the bomb groups in that organisation. A single letter group identification marking would appear in the symbol, for example, 'A' for the 44th Bomb Group; 'B' for the 93rd Bomb Group and 'C' for the 389th, etc.

The Dreamboat, converted from the B-17E 41-9112, was far from that, as it was a heavy aeroplane, unpopular with those who flew it, and the programme was abandoned.

A taxiing accident on 17 April 1944 cost the life of a civilian contractor who was riding in the passenger seat of the lorry. Tail-wheel aircraft such as the P-51 were notoriously difficult to taxi.

The 44th Bomb Group's B-24J 42-100400, which sought neutrality at Dübendorf, Switzerland on 18 March 1944, after being hit in three engines during a raid on Friedrichshafen. Just three days before, the aircraft had left Warton for its return to the Group after a complete overhaul.

The Mustang's long nose and restricted vision while taxiing caused yet another accident when a new P-51B ploughed into a parked aircraft. Almost half of the unfortunate aeroplane's port wing had disappeared before the crew chief could stop his charge.

A number of Tiger Moths were used by the 8th Air Force. This example retained its RAF markings although it had already gained a shark's mouth design on the nose. In the background is the 4th Fighter Group's Airspeed Oxford, AS728, with a P-47 Thunderbolt in the distance.

Fay Brandis flies this P-51B between Warton's control tower and the hangars during a mock attack exercise on 21 March 1944. The Mustang 43-12177 was later transferred to the RAF, becoming SR414.

An exciting shot of BAD.2's B-26 Marauder *Demon Deacon*, piloted by Major Joe Stenglein, CO of the 310th Ferry Squadron, seen during the attack exercise.

The nose art of *Demon Deacon* shows a holy man chasing a naked young lady! In the photograph are, from left to right: Major Norman Isenberg; Sergeant Ray Dlouhy, crew chief; Captain Fay Brandis, regular pilot and Captain Bob Forehand, engineering officer. The Marauder served Warton for most of the unit's existence before being flown to Germany for scrapping at the end of the war.

The B-17F *Black Diamond Express*, a famous aircraft of the 303rd Bomb Group, staged through Warton on its return to the United States on 30 March 1944. The aircraft was covered with hundreds of names and messages from the personnel of the 303rd before it departed from its base at Molesworth.

Heavy fog at Warton forced test pilot Jack Knight to divert his B-17 to Squires Gate airfield at Blackpool. As the weather was little better there the Fortress skidded onto the grass. There was a happy ending for Knight and engineer Spence Thwaites as, a few yards further on, the aircraft would have ended up in a large open cesspool!

In pristine condition and ready for delivery, a B-24 tops up with fuel before its flight to East Anglia to join the war.

The main hangar area at Warton as seen on 23 April 1944, with a large number and variety of aircraft types visible. In the foreground B-24s await delivery, while outside Hangars 6 and 7, to the right, all of the main fighter types are being readied for flight test. On the ramp near the control tower are P-51s for processing as well as a number of visitors, including a Mosquito and an Anson.

Battle damaged aircraft often looked worse when the engineers involved in the repair had to tear away some of the aircraft's structure, as on the wing of this B-24.

A meeting was held at the start of every shift. Major Gale E. Schooling, head of Flight Test gives his section's briefing. In the background are a P-47 Thunderbolt and an ex-RAF Lockheed Hudson, one of a number transferred to the 8th AFSC for light transport duties.

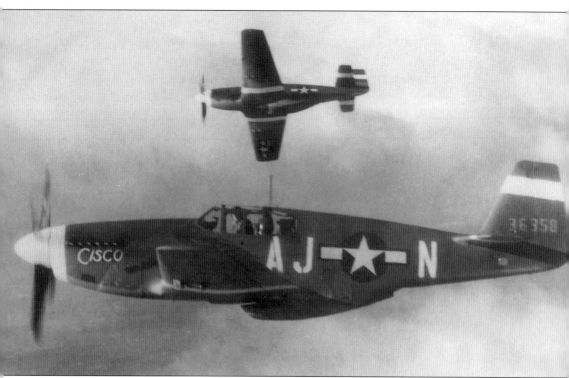

BAD.2's chief test pilot, Charles Himes, flies the P-51B 43-3658 soon after it arrived at Warton for overhaul and reallocation. The aircraft has the markings of the 354th Fighter Group but, after processing, it was transferred to the 4th Fighter Group at Debden in Essex. Its career ended in Italy as spares for Mustangs of the 325th Fighter Group.

Thunderbolts still turned up at Warton for processing despite that task being allocated to Burtonwood. As the 8th Air Force fighter groups were being re-equipped with the P-51 to replace the big fighter, P-47s were being allocated to the 9th Air Force as fighter-bombers.

Another task for Warton's Alert Crew as the B-24 *Lancashire Lass* ends up in the grass after a tyre burst on landing. Besides the difficulty in moving the aircraft, incidents like this could affect the flying programme.

P-51s in natural metal finish started to arrive at Warton in February 1944, the aircraft receiving black identification bands over the wings and tail surfaces during their processing. With the earlier olive drab coloured aircraft the bands were in white but, later in the war, the painting of these markings were dispensed with.

The Flight Test hangars were always busy, with aircraft being made available for check flights at a rapid rate. Here P-47s and P-51s await their turn while the larger aircraft, normally parked on the ramp, are in whatever space was available!

On 30 May 1944 a ceremony was held to mark the purchase of three P-51s by the personnel of BAD.2. The target of two aircraft was exceeded by enough money to buy the third. In the distant mist a natural metal finished B-17G in RAF roundels can be seen.

The troops turned out in force for the P-51 war bond ceremony, with the Mustangs being named *Pride of the Yanks*, *Too Bad* and *Mazie R*, the latter being named in honour of the mother of one of the men who picked the name after winning a draw.

Test pilot Jack Knight flies this new P-51B above the Lancashire overcast on 31 May 1944. Many of the American pilots, who had trained in the clear blue skies over Arizona and the like, received quite a shock when they had to come to terms with the British weather.

Hangar 1 was used for storage until a steady stream of new aircraft forced the need for its intended use. Even then some machines were worked upon in the open, providing the weather was kind.

Despite the best efforts of the controllers, taxiing accidents on a busy airfield are always a possibility. A visiting Miles Master II, AZ600, collided with a stationary jeep, without injury apart from the pilot's dented pride.

Having been completely overhauled, this B-24 is being towed out of Hangar 4 by tractor driver Frank Segalle. After being flight tested the aircraft would be made available for delivery to an operational unit.

As one aircraft goes out another takes its place, being towed in for processing at the opposite end of Hangar 4. A B-24 enters the hangar from the control tower ramp while the new P-51s await their turn to go into Hangar 5 next door.

A general view of Hangar 5 in mid-1944, showing accommodation for over twenty Mustangs. The following photograph makes an interesting 'Then and Now' comparison.

An Open Day at Warton, fifty-five years later, shows that Hangar 4 still houses fine aircraft but this time the occupants are British Aerospace Hawks. This shot shows that the layout has changed little although the blacked-out windows in the wartime picture are now clear.

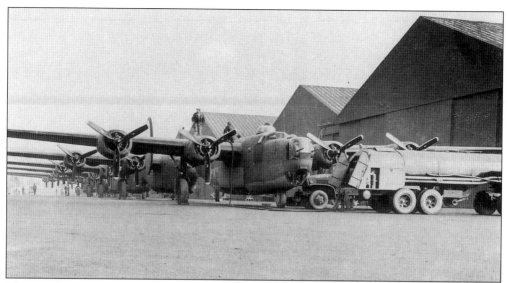

The continuous and ever-changing line-up of B-24s parked at the rear of the main hangars left little room for manoeuvre when other aircraft had to be moved around.

The famous film actor James Stewart served as a squadron commander with the 445th Bomb Group at Tibenham, Norfolk. Here, with members of his crew, he poses near the B-24 *Male Call*, which he piloted on a number of missions. Despite his fame Stewart did not shirk his responsibilities, flying twenty combat operations before being transferred to the 453rd Bomb Group as group operations officer. After the war Stewart's service record rated him as 'Superior'. The aircraft was overhauled at Warton at a later date but the engineers were unaware of its famous pilot.

The Operations Room at Warton was the nerve centre of all flight movements, both in and out of the airfield. Maps and charts cover the walls with the chalk board showing changes in radio frequencies, code-words and emergency procedures. Hanging from the ceiling of the Operations Room are a number of recognition models, including Japanese types!

The Russian visitor studying the work sheet for the P-51B 42-106683, although in civilian clothes, was later found to be a general! Lower ranked officers in the Soviet Air Force delegation to BAD.2 wore their normal uniforms. The inspected aircraft later became SR423, a Mustang III of the RAF.

Three
The Pressure Mounts

Jack Knight took this photograph showing the Nissen Huts of Site 10, left, and Site 11 in the centre of the picture. The village of Freckleton, which would be the scene of a disastrous aircraft accident, is to the right of the photograph.

A milestone for Hangar 4 was the 500th B-24 Liberator to be completed. Sergeant Howard Tice has the honour of towing the Winged Fury from the hangar while, in true military tradition, the aircraft's paperwork is being passed by Technical Sergeant Keller to Captain Ora Bard.

Orville Wrosch drives one of the many Cletracs, used by the USAAF on bases throughout the world. The tractor was particularly useful for towing out aircraft which had become bogged down in the mud after going off the runway or taxi track.

A number of British-built Miles Master trainers were supplied to the 8th Air Force for communications work. Lieutenants Guinn and Threadwell pose at Warton with one of this type showing the star and bar insignia painted over the RAF roundel.

One of BAD.2's many specialised sections was the Armament Department and here the gun turret repair crews are at work repairing scrapped or damaged turrets during a shortage of such in the middle of 1944.

Engine mechanics steam clean the number one engine of the 446th Bomb Group's *The Spirit of 77*, which had flown on eighty-one missions by the time it arrived at Warton for overhaul.

Scene of the night shift working on the new B-24s in Hangar 4. Some of the engineers preferred to work during the night time but every man knew the operation completed by the previous team and the work carried on continuously.

Flight Test's Bob Kitch, Frank Segalle and Orville Wrosch break for a photograph while working on a new P-51B outside Hangar 6.

Supervising the undercarriage retraction tests on a B-24 in Hangar 4 is Staff Sergeant Tony Piscattelli, who became Chief of Police for Elizabethtown, Pennsylvania in the 1960s.

The undercarriage legs of a B-24 weighed over a quarter of a ton, with the removal taking five men over four hours but, in a method devised by Master Sergeant Fred Covert, the whole operation was reduced to half the man-hours with only two men completing the work. The ingenuity of the BAD.2 technicians in the various sections cut down working time in many areas.

The Liberator's massive Pratt & Whitney R-1830 radial engines nearly filled the engine nacelle but some cowlings were detachable, while other parts folded, making access fairly simple. However, because of the compactness, the mechanics suffered many scraped knuckles!

Ladders and makeshift stands had to be used to reach the bomber's engines and propellers until safer platforms were manufactured by the maintenance people.

The strengthening of the taxi track around the airfield's perimeter caused a big headache for Flight Operations and the air traffic people. Here a contractor's steamroller crawled along in front of a B-24 for ten minutes before turning off the taxi track to allow the bomber to pass.

This B-17's stay at Warton was much longer than expected after it had nosed over while crossing the main runway. The crew chief at the controls thought he saw another aircraft coming in to land and stood hard on the brakes, forcing the machine to stand on its nose which was completely crumpled. As no aircraft was landing the unfortunate sergeant was teased by his colleagues that he must have seen a seagull!

A regular sight in the streets of Liverpool were the convoys of American aircraft leaving the docks for their journey to Speke airfield for assembly. The P-51Ds passing the Plaza cinema in Allerton Road were soon on their way from Speke to Warton.

After their arrival at Warren the new P-51Ds were soon in the air after processing, which included a dorsal fillet addition to the fin to improve longitudinal stability, as the rear fuselage had less area after the introduction of the clear-view canopy.

The bubble-canopy version of the P-47D Thunderbolt started to appear in England in May 1944 and this photograph captures the moment when a convoy from the docks starts to turn at Princess Park Gates, Liverpool. The policeman is making sure that nothing gets in the way of the war effort, not even a tram!

A short time later the Thunderbolts had been processed by BAD.1 at Burtonwood and are lined up awaiting delivery to their respective units. There were four P-47 groups operating in the 8th Air Force at the time of D-Day as the fighter units were standardizing with the Mustang. By the war's end only the 56th Fighter Group flew Thunderbolts in the 8th Air Force, as most of this type had been transferred to the 9th Air Force for the fighter-bomber role.

Test pilot Bill Watters awaits start-up clearance for the P-51D 44-13590 and still wears the lightweight helmet he brought with him from the United States.

The urgent requirement for extra storage space saw the construction of a number of warehouses for the Supplies Department. The new buildings were almost ready for occupation when the photograph was taken on 18 July 1944.

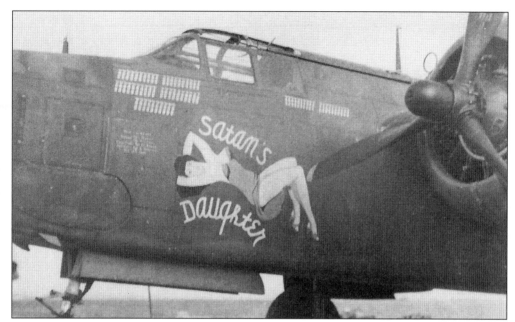

Arriving at Warton for overhaul, this A-20G Havoc *Satan's Daughter* was a veteran with seventy missions completed. The three groups operating A-20s in the 9th Air Force were used in the light bomber role until their gradual replacement by the excellent A-26 Invader.

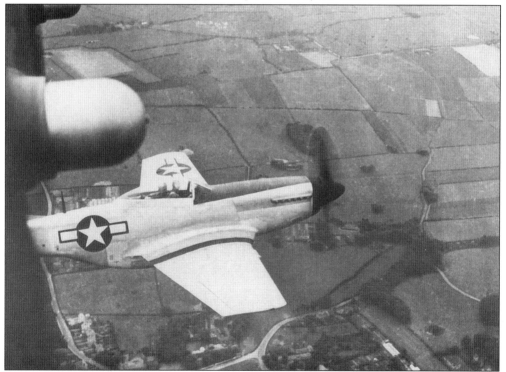

Photographed by Jack Knight from the pilot's seat of a B-24, the P-51D is flown by Lt Bill Clearwater. Clearwater was to lose his life a few days later in the crash of 44-13403 after a wing detached from the aircraft.

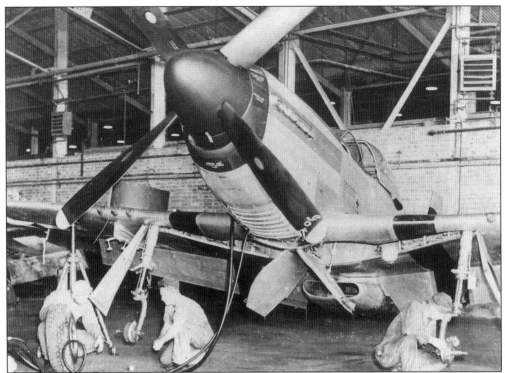

After the tragic crash of the Mustang flown by Clearwater, to be followed by another fatal accident in similar circumstances, in which test pilot Burtie Orth was killed, it was left to the BAD.2 technicians to find the cause. A P-51D was thoroughly tested at Warton and the mystery solved, no doubt saving the lives of many Mustang pilots in the future.

The beautiful Mosquito XVI looks sad after this wheels-up landing on 17 June 1944. Flown by chief test pilot Charlie Himes, the aircraft had a complete electrical failure on approach to Warton's Runway 08, ending up in the bushes near Site 9. Luckily, there were no injuries to Himes or co-pilot John Bloemendal.

Warton's hangars and technical area, photographed in the summer of 1944, show a vast assortment of aircraft types, including two of the black painted 'Carpetbagger' B-24 Liberators.

The Packard-Merlin engine assembly line looks busy with both Packard and Rolls-Royce always in attendance. The engine specialists had an excellent record with very few failures during the test runs before installation into an aircraft.

Midnite Mistress, the all-black B-24 flown by the Special Operations Group or 'Carpetbaggers'. At the time of this photograph in July 1944, the unit, the 801st Bomb Group, was based at Harrington in Northamptonshire, mainly flying missions in support of the resistance movements in Europe. After completing over sixty operations this aircraft had returned to BAD.2 for overhaul.

Another 'Carpetbagger' to return to Warton for overhaul was *Tiger's Revenge*, a B-24H which had over 1,000 flying hours to its credit. During the last winter of the war night-bombing missions were undertaken, until March 1945 when the Group returned to its special activities.

A-20 Havocs, with both solid and bombardier-type noses, ready for their return to the light bomb groups of the 9th Air Force after overhaul. These aircraft would serve until replaced by A-26 Invaders, with the first unit, the 416th Bomb Group, receiving the new type in November 1944.

The rebuilt P-51B *Spare Parts* was classed as a write-off when it was dropped while being unloaded from a freighter at Liverpool docks in February 1944. Just five months later the Mustang was flying again as a 'hack' for BAD.2, operating on many 'morale-boosting' missions.

This dramatic photograph of *Spare Parts* was taken over the Welsh mountains, en route to Exeter aerodrome, with one of the ferry pilots in the rear seat. Test pilot Joe Bosworth had been detailed to make the flight for his passenger to bring a stranded aircraft back to Warton.

A close-up of 43-6623's glamorous nose art, painted after a vote was taken on what type of design would be appropriate! The aircraft was parked outside Flight Test's Nissen Hut operations office next to Hangar 6.

Ray Dloughy fuels up *Spare Parts* before another important mission to an airfield near to a Scottish whisky distillery! Converted to a two-seater, the aeroplane also gave many of the ground crew a chance to fly in a fighter.

The pressure of work and long hours on duty after the D-Day Invasion took its toll on everyone and short breaks had to be taken whenever possible. Ray Dloughy grabs a few minutes rest while working on the B-24J 42-51435 in August 1944.

The modified interior of a B-24 'Carpetbagger'. Plywood floors were fitted over the aircraft's structure and seats installed for the use of agents or other passengers on less dangerous missions.

Captain Glenn Miller posed with Major Fred Jacobs and a Clark Gable look-alike, who travelled with the band, near the B-24 *Donna Mia* after arriving at Warton on 13 August 1944. Major Jacobs, of the 310th Ferry Squadron, had the honour of pinning the Oak Leaves rank insignia on Glenn Miller when the latter's promotion to Major was confirmed.
(Photo: Edward F. Polic).

The Aircraft Salvage Department saved the U.S. taxpayers thousands of dollars by removing just about everything possible from an aeroplane during the scrapping process. This A-20 is receiving their full attention although the teams had only just started!

Four

The Frecklton Disaster and Beyond

Only nine days after the visit of Glenn Miller's band Warton was in the news again but for a much different reason. A severe electrical storm had caught the B-24 Liberator 42-50291 duringthe landing approach after a test flight, causing it to crash onto the infant's section of the Holy Trinity School in Freckleton. The photograph shows the crash site, with one of the aircraft's main wheels lying amongst the blazing wreckage.

Local volunteers, police and personnel from Warton probe the disaster area for signs of life and, although some children were rescued, the death toll eventually reached sixty-one, including the three man crew of the B-24.

A stark reminder of the crash, one of the B-24's main undercarriage legs lies on the pavement near Freckleton's village green.

The continuous line of P-51D Mustangs never seemed to diminish as, when one was taken away on delivery, another rolled out of Hangar 5 to take its place. The nearest aircraft in this picture, 44-13982, joined the 20th Fighter Group at Kings Cliffe, Northamptonshire, where it became known as *Maggie*.

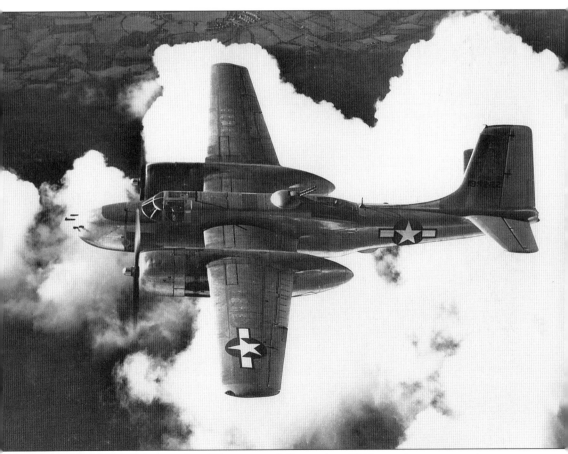

The first A-26 Invader arrived at Warton on 4 September 1944, causing great excitement among both air and ground crews as advanced word had been received telling them of the atrcraft's potential. They were not deceived, as the Invader proved itself to be a fine machine, serving with the U.S. Air Force in the Second World War, Korean and Vietnam wars.

In a strange combination this B-17F *Maid To Take It!* was converted to the transport configuration at BAD.1 at Burtonwood, although on this visit to Warton the aircraft appears to have the Norden bombsight cover in place. A P-38 Lightning can be seen in the background.

In common with other new P-51Ds, 44-14244 wore the black nose as painted at the air depot, but all would carry different colours after joining their respective units. This aeroplane was about to join the 356th Fighter Group at Martlesham, Suffolk, to carry their distinctive blue and red diamond pattern.

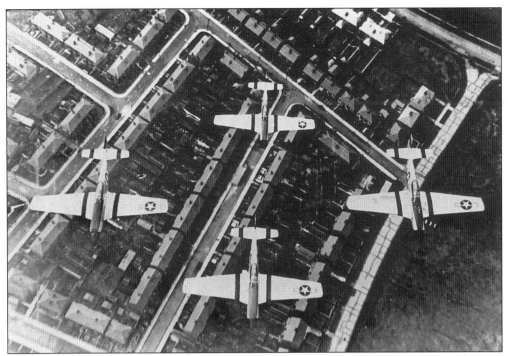

While the new Mustangs were waiting to be delivered, the Warton test pilots took every opportunity to practise their formation flying, here photographed flying low over the streets of Lytham. They would then change positions to echelon to fly over the airfield and peel up to decrease speed before getting into the circuit for a stream landing.

Another great morale boost was the visit on 1 September 1944 of 'The Old Groaner' himself, Bing Crosby. He performed for longer than the allocated time, singing many requests for the Warton troops but he also found the time to visit the station's hospital to sing to some of the survivors of the Freckleton air crash. He was photographed leaving the base theatre by Les Smith, a young RAF airman serving at Warton.

Peter Manaserro flies one of the new A-26s over the outskirts of Preston on his way back to Warton after a test flight. A test pilot of great experience, Manaserro was killed after the war while testing an F-86 Sabre jet fighter.

One of the P-38 Lightnings returning to BAD No.2 for overhaul was the P-38J 44-23152 named *The Virgin*. With no mission markings or victory symbols on its nose it would appear that the aircraft was well named.

The rear of the main hangars, photographed as the L-4 circled the technical area, with B-24s and A-20s much in evidence. In the foreground are a couple of P-38s, an AT-6 and a UC-64 Norseman is behind the Flight Test hangars.

With the large number of flying hours accumulated after the Invasion it was not surprising that aircraft were returning from the combat groups for complete overhauls less than three months after leaving Warton on their initial delivery. Here *Dopey Gal*, from the 9th Air Force's 363rd Fighter Group, had returned from their base at Azeville, France and waits with other P-51s for its turn through Hangar 5. The 363rd became a Tactical Reconnaissance Group during September 1944.

An excellent view of the hangars and ramp in September 1944 shows six of the newly arrived A-26s outside the main production hangars. Note the shadow of the L-4 Grasshopper from which this shot was taken.

Test pilot Jack Knight loved to fly and qualified on no less than twenty-five types during his war service. His off-duty time was spent visiting as many English towns as possible but it was not all play as he flew 1,166 times during his two years at Warton.

The predominantly Mustang flight-line finds space for two P-38s, while outside Hangars 6 and 7 there is room for one Hudson among the P-51s. In the distance B-24s are parked in the Bank Lane dispersal area, where the author spent most of his school vacations viewing the activities of BAD.2.

Besides the fitting of armour plating to the sides of the cockpit to protect the pilots, the most common modification to the B-24s was the installation of a blister window on each side of the nose to assist the navigator. The combat experience of Liberator groups forced a long list of modifications to be implemented at BAD.2, adding to the already extensive overhaul programmes.

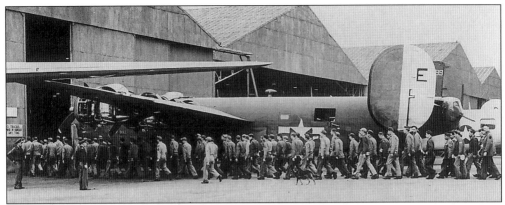

The morning shift marches into Hangar 4 past the waiting B-24J 42-51289, which has returned to Warton from the 34th Bomb Group at Mendlesham, Suffolk, after that unit had exchanged its Liberators for B-17G Fortresses. The B-24 would be reassigned to another group which had retained that type.

An unusual visitor to Warton was 43-48526, a radar-equipped C-47B from the 9th Troop Carrier Command's Pathfinder School. Twenty of these pathfinder aircraft were the first American types to take part in the D-Day Invasion.

As a result of the shortage of transport aircraft in the 8th Air Force, besides the B-17s, a number of B-24 Liberators were also converted for that role. A transparent nose replaced the front gun turret, as seen in this photograph of an aircraft parked on the north side of Hangar 1. Other conversions for weather and night-leaflet aircraft were also completed.

Peter Manaserro and Jack Knight 'volunteered' to deliver this new A-26 to Melun for the 416th Bomb Group after a shortage of ferry pilots required off-duty test pilots to fly the aircraft. It was no surprise that the 416th's airfield just happened to be near Paris, with the possibility of a few days in the French capital proving to be a great attraction.

The B-17G 42-97108, after conversion to the transport role as a CB-108. The aircraft, which was destined for the RAF as HB771, was transferred to the USAAF after the former's need for Fortresses diminished. Used by the 8th AFSC, it was unusual in having invasion stripes applied, as these were not normally carried by the heavier types.

The Canadian-built Noordyne UC-64 Norseman was the workhorse of the light transport types. Too noisy to be used by VIPs, the aircraft had a large cabin area and its rugged construction made it capable of landing on the roughest of airstrips.

Sixty-seven of the Stinson L-5 Sentinel liaison aircraft were assembled at Warton. This example 42-99081 was attached to the 406th Bomb Squadron, a 'Carpetbagger' unit based at Harrington, Northamptonshire.

The B-24L 44-49359, which had been converted to a transport aircraft, wears the code-letters of the 32nd Transport Squadron of the 9th Air Force, although there is no listing of the type in the unit records. It is possible that the aircraft was used for training its pilots to fly fuel-carrying missions.

P-51Ds from the 55th Fighter Group at Wormingford, Essex, lined up on Warton's ramp after arriving at BAD.2 for an engine change. The nearest aircraft is named *Alice Marie II*.

The first of three accidents which took place on 5 October 1944, when a change to the short runway by high winds saw this B-24J 44-40466, arriving from the 466th Bomb Group at Attlebridge, Norfolk, skidd off the runway.

Doing his best to avoid the crashed B-24, this A-20 Pilot took his aeroplane even further off the runway. The A-20K 44-561 was repaired and flew again, only to join others for scrapping later in the war!

The dreaded Runway 15/33 added this Mustang to its accident total for 5th October, as the ferry pilot bringing the brand new P-51D from Speke, Liverpool, ground-looped his mount to avoid hitting the other two bent aeroplanes.

The new Mustang should have joined these recently delivered machines waiting outside Hangar 5. The nearest aircraft, 44-14182, joined the 353rd Fighter Group at Raydon in Essex after completing its processing at BAD.2

Warton ferry pilot George Batchelor was forced to land this P-38J Lightning at Langley, Buckinghamshire, after engine trouble on a ferry flight from the Continent to BAD.1 at Burtonwood. The private airfield was owned by Hawker Aircraft Limited and one of the company's policemen guards the aircraft until repairs can be made.

Conversions of the Fortress were popular with those who flew them, as the removal of the gun turrets and weight saving made the aircraft into a 'hot ship', adding up to thirty miles an hour to the speed. The B-17G *Flak Hopper* had been badly damaged on its fourteenth mission and was allocated for conversion during the repairs.

A newly dug drainage ditch caused this accident to the A-26 when the brakes failed while negotiating a corner of the taxi track. There were recriminations afterwards as the contractors had failed to inform Base Operations of their work. The picture is also of interest as it shows that underwing gun packs had been fitted to this aircraft.

Heading for home! Major Himes pilots the C-47B 43-48770, borrowed from the 27th Air Transport Group, back to Warton after a liaison flight to units in East Anglia.

Stretching completely around Warton's perimeter track a row of A-26s Invaders await collection. Deliveries to the combat units went smoothly until 29 November 1944 when two of the aircraft collided soon after take-off. Sadly, both crews died.

For some reason this small house was allowed to remain standing in the south-eastern corner of the airfield while others were demolished during the construction of the aerodrome in 1940. The house remains to this day, decorated with its original wallpaper!

Another of the 801st Bomb Group's 'Carpetbagger' Liberators was this B-24H 42-50682, seen after its return to Warton for battle damage repairs.

A war-weary C-47, named *Chukky*, arrived at BAD.2 for scrapping but some of the Hangar 4 personnel thought that it was too good to be broken-up and asked permission to restore the aircraft in their own time as they did with the P-51 *Spare Parts*.

The C-47 *Chukky*, 41-38607, was completely stripped down and rebuilt where it stood in Hangar 4. After much hard work the aircraft emerged as *Jackpot*, named in honour of Head of Maintenance, Colonel Paul Jackson who, in 1941, was one of the USAAF pilots who had cleared the type for military service.

A line-up including *Jackpot*, an A-20 Havoc and the AT-6D 42-85163, which was originally known as *Hoodwink* but later assumed the name *Jet Threat*.

From an Ugly Duckling to a Beautiful Swan! An excellent shot of *Jackpot* on the flight-line. The Warton engineers did a fine job, as the aircraft flew for many years after the war.

Some of Warton's Flight Test pilots with the station 'hack' aircraft including:
The P-47 *El Champo*, C-47 *Jackpot*, P-51 *Spare Parts* and AT-6 *Jet Threat*. Out of the picture was the UC-78 *Bamboo Bomber*.

A Chevrolet van was the standard vehicle for use on runway control duty and it was a lonely vigil for those parked near the end of the active runway. A B-24 top turret provides the observation dome as a P-51 roars away for take-off from a wintry Warton.

The exchange of the aircraft's papers after completion by Hangar 4 meant that the B-24L 44-49591 was cleared for flight testing. On 15 December 1944 the name *One Grand* was painted on the nose of the Liberator as the 1,000th aircraft to be processed by that hangar.

Outside, the Hangar 4 personnel gather around *One Grand* for a souvenir photograph. After the flight tests were completed the aircraft was delivered to the 467th Bomb Group at Rackheath, Norfolk but the name was removed before leaving, as its new crew would no doubt want their own name for the aeroplane.

Five
Victory In Sight

BAD.2's own UC-64 Norseman, which had played the leading part in a strange story. The aircraft was stolen by one of the mechanics who had heard that his brother was in France serving in the US Army and hatched a plan to fly the Norseman over to join him. His navigation let him down because he thought that Angelsey was France and landed at RAF Valley, only to be arrested and eventually court marshalled. Warton's Air Traffic Control had been particularly busy, so one more aircraft taking-off would not have aroused suspicion.

The Warton ramp displays its usual variety of aircraft, including two A-20s of the 416th Bomb Group which had returned to BAD.2 after that unit had been re-equipped with the A-26 Invader. Outside Hangar 7 is *Jackpot* with another C-47, while in the foreground is a visiting Norseman. In the distance are parked B-24s and an A-26 in Dispersal Area No.1, which was the author's vantage point on his many trips to Warton.

A wintry scene on Warton's ramp which shows an interesting visitor in the shape of a Northrop P-61 Black Widow night fighter. The aircraft had arrived from its base in France for a liaison visit to BAD.1 at Burtonwood, followed by the short flight to BAD.2. The P-61 returned to its base at Rouvres after its crew spent three evenings in Blackpool!

The snow-covered technical area in February 1945 has the usual B-24s, while a Hudson is outside Hangar 4 and a C-47 waits near Flight Test's Hangar 7. In the foreground is the outline in the snow of a recently parked C-47 in front of Hangar 9.

The arrival at Warton of one of the RAF's Gloster Meteor prototypes caused much excitement among BAD.2's air minded personnel. The pilots hung on every word as the RAF pilot described jet flight. American offers to try out the aircraft were politely rejected.

A C-47 was specially painted for 'Operation Bear Hug', the transportation of gifts to the RAF station at Ford in Sussex for distribution to Russian ex-POWs who were accommodated in an army camp near Worthing. The aircraft's crew members had to run the gauntlet of Russian kisses!

The nose insignia of a 436th Troop Carrier Group C-47. It was one of the many which arrived at Warton to tow away the gliders covering the airfield. The code 'S6' shows that the aircraft belonged to the 79th Squadron.

Aviation enthusiast and test pilot, Jack Knight always took a camera into the air with him and could not resist photographing the Royal Navy Fairey Firefly I, Z1977, of No.1771 Squadron flying from Burscough, near Southport.

The assembly of a Waco CG-4 glider required a lot of muscle and some strong backs, shown here as the folding cockpit section is fitted to the fuselage.

Unsung, but no less important, were BAD.2's fuel tanker drivers. The centre vehicle is an Autocar tractor unit with a 4,000 US gallons tanker, with the tanker on the left having a Biederman F-1 unit. Warton had fifteen such tankers.

A photograph of the technical area also shows over forty C-47s, some on Runway 02/20 while others line the perimeter track, awaiting their turn to enter the main runway and glider attachment before take-off.

Still they come! *Nancy M. 2nd*, a blue-nosed P-51D of the 352nd Fighter Group at Bodney, Norfolk, joined the queue of Mustangs awaiting overhaul. Note the exhaust streaks along the fuselage.

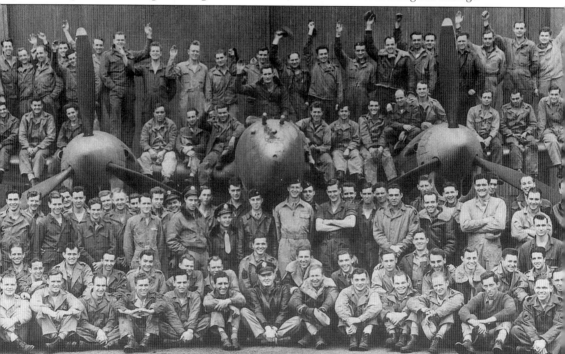

A Lockheed P-38 Lightning provided the photo platform for the Flight Test team. Under the aircraft's nose, wearing his flight overalls, is chief test pilot Major Charles Himes, to his right is Captain Tom Boland, the engineering officer, while sitting directly in front is test pilot Jack Knight. On the extreme right in his A-2 jacket is test pilot Wally Woltemath.

The 'V4' coded C-47s are from the 304th Squadron of the 442nd TCG. Lead aircraft *V-Victor* was flown by the Group Commander, Colonel Charles M. Smith.

The Waco CG-4s, with tow-lines already attached, wait to be hooked up to the C-47s for their flight across the Channel to bases in France.

Orville Wrosch relaxes in the spring sunshine during April 1945. The visiting B-26 Marauder coded 'VT-N' is from the 453rd Squadron of the 323rd Bomb Group who, at that time, were based at Prouvy airfield, near Denain in Northern France.

The nose of a new visitor to Warton in the shape of the Douglas C-54 Skymaster 42-72309. After the war the aircraft would be converted to the civilian airliner NC90434, operating for many years with American Airlines.

The wheels are starting to lower for landing on the B-17G 43-38190 as Mike Murtha pilots the aircraft over the Ribble mudflats. In the distance, to the left of the picture, is the town of Lytham.

Flight engineer Spence Thwaites checks the engines of one of the C-47s before it is returned to its group. The elaborately painted cowlings were red and yellow.

BAD.2 test pilot Pete Swank was ordered to France to bring back this C-47 to Warton for overhaul. Unfortunately, before he arrived at Prosnes, France, the aircraft, which belonged to the 90th Squadron of the 438th Troop Carrier Group, had been damaged in a landing accident.

Showing its neutral colours, an Irish vessel sails up the River Ribble to Preston docks. As the ship passes Warton, the then new Hangars 31 and 32 can be seen on the right of the photograph, while hundreds of aircraft can be seen on the airfield, including an RAF Handley Page Halifax of Coastal Command.

On final approach to Runway 26, with wheels down and flaps yet to be lowered, the Fortress roars in to Warton.

Pete Swank brings the A-20K 44-560 back to Warton after a flight to BAD.3 at Langford Lodge, Northern Ireland. Nearing Blackpool the famous central pier, Winter Gardens and the railway station can all be seen in this photograph.

This photograph of flight engineer Spence Thwaites is interesting because of the C-47 in the background carrying the code-letters 'PJ' as the identity of the unit is unknown. No official listing of aircraft codes exists but it is thought that these letters and 'PK' were used by the 302nd Air Transport Wing.

An AT-24, the courier version of the B-25 Mitchell bomber, taxies out after a VIP visit. In the foreground is BAD.2's UC-78 *Bamboo Bomber*; parked outside Hangar 1 is the B-17G 44-6169.

This was the news that everyone was waiting for, with officers and enlisted men sharing the great joy of the defeat of Germany. However for some this news was tempered by the thoughts of being transferred to the Pacific for the war against Japan.

The newly overhauled C-47s were immediately pressed into service after their flight test clearance, carrying supplies directly to the continent. The aircraft 43-48884, loading 110 gallon, US-made drop tanks, appears to have been fitted with a new port wing. The large sports field in the distance is now the site of a large assembly hangar for BAE Systems.

Six

The Run Down

One of the Alert Crew sections, with their officer Lt Tom Flowers, pose with their yellow and black chequered jeeps and one of their charges. The fifty calibre nose armament of the A-26 Invader is evident in this photograph.

The Engine Test Department proudly displays the notice of their achievements in the Rolls-Royce Packard Merlin section, which had a fine record with this excellent engine. Besides this total, a further 2,586 Allison V-1710s were processed and, before standardization to in-line engines, 126 radials were also completed.

A heavy landing caused the undercarriage to collapse, forcing this A-20 off the runway and into the corn stooks. A ferry pilot had flown the aircraft to BAD.2 for disposal but seems to have saved the Salvage Department some work.

The parked A-20G, 43-9384, along with other Havocs, had arrived at Warton for scrapping but not for demolishing by a Liberator, although the end result would be the same! Note the Curriss C-46 Commando aircraft parked outside the main hangars in this photograph taken on 17 July 1945.

The offending B-24J, 42-51523, had served with the 458th Bomb Group before returning to BAD.2 for the redeployment project. A failure of the starboard undercarriage leg caused the accident.

Returning to where they started, aircraft began to arrive at Speke, Liverpool, for their journey to the docks and return to the United States in a complete reversal of how they arrived. The P-51Ds, *Passion's Playground* and *Elionne*, were flown by Captain Herbert G. Marsh of the 355th Fighter Group based at Steeple Morden, Cambridgeshire.

This veteran P-38 Lightning was a source of great interest with its tally of missions and victories adorning the nose. All of these made no difference to the final outcome as the scrap-man got it in the end.

Outlined in chalk especially for the photograph, this impression in the concrete of one of Warton's hangars is a poignant reminder of BAD.2's occupation. It is still a source of great interest for visitors to the site.

A souvenir photograph of the Alert Crew at the war's end. The team, which had worked so well together for over two years, would now be dispersing, with most of them returning to their homes in the United States. Byron Amundsen, sitting on the jeep's bumper, provided this treasured photograph.

The standard equipment for the 86th Fighter Group was the P-47 Thunderbolt. This aircraft of the 526th Squadron joined others in the Lansberg line-up to become the victim of a giant blade which was dropped by crane to slice off the engines.

Another 'hack' of the 86th Fighter Group was the veteran B-26 Marauder 42-107488 which was flown in from Italy to face the chop. It was a sad task for the engineers who had supplied much tender loving care to keep the aircraft flying. Warton Personnel were transfered to Germany to assist with the demolition.

Warton airfield photographed on 1 July 1974 gives an excellent impression of its wartime layout, as the post-war runway extensions are not in the picture. The hangars remain the same, but BAD.2's Runway 15/33 has now been changed to 14/32.

Seven

B-24 Liberator Nose-Art

Old Baldy of the 93rd Bomb Group based at Hardwick, Norfolk.

Shoo-Shoo Baby showing the 'Flying Eight Ball' insignia of the 44th Bomb Group which operated from Shipham, Norfolk.

The Queen of Hearts, 42-52511, of the 466th Bomb Group, was not able to return to its base at Attlebridge, Norfolk, as its days were ended by a crash-landing at New Romney, Kent, after a mission on 17 July 1944.

This aircraft's name *Wham! Bam! Thank You Mam* has a number of connotations! Flown by the 491st from Metfield, Suffolk, the serial number was 42-110107.

Flying from Debach, Suffolk, *The Wild Hare* served with the 493rd Bomb Group until that unit was re-equipped with B-17s late in August 1944.

Another of the Attlebridge based B-24s was *Betta Duck*, number 44-49454, which survived the war while serving with the 466th Bomb Group.

The 34th Bomb Group's *Misschief* arrived at Warton from its base at Mendlesham in Suffolk for reassignment, after that unit had changed to the B-17 in August 1944.

Number 42-92536 had a Baseball term, *You're Safe at Home,* for its name.

The *Play Boy* of the 466th Bomb Group left its base at Attlebridge on 29 April 1944 for an attack on the Friedrichstrasse railway station in Berlin. However, this aircraft, 41-29399, ended its career in Holland after being shot down by a combination of flak and fighters.

Times A'Wastin' flew its last mission on 5 September 1944 when the 466th took part in a raid on the railway yards at Karlsruhe, Germany. No.42-50569 was heavily damaged by flak and, after an emergency landing in England, the aircraft never flew again.

Arriving at Warton from its base at Seething, Norfolk, *Back to the Sack*, of the 448th Bomb Group, shows its nose art in full. Unfortunately, after the fitment of the armoured panels to the cockpit sides, some of Donald's beak and his candle were lost!

The fitting of the side armour at BAD.2 also took away some of the painting of Desperate Desmond, Belonging to the 446th Bomb Group at Bungay, Suffolk, the aircraft was 42-7498.

Another of the 448th's aircraft flown into Warton for modification and overhaul was *Reddy Teddy*. This aircraft also returned to Seething minus some of its nose art.

Flying from North Pickenham after the 491st's move from Metfield, the *Heavenly Body* retained its painting after the attachment of the cockpit armour, with the co-pilot already adding his name to the new addition. The serial number was 42-110155.

Ten Gun Dottie operated from Horsham St Faith (now Norwich Airport) with the 755th Squadron of the 458th Bomb Group. The position of the cockpit armour is well illustrated. This photo was taken after a mission to the Misburg oil installations on 26 November 1944.

Dorty Treek of the 491st Bomb Group, based at North Pickenham, had to be abandoned over Belgium after being hit by flak.

The changeover from B-24s to B-17s for the 493rd at Debach left *Hairless Joe* looking for another group after arriving at BAD.2 for overhaul and reassignment. Sometimes the aircraft name was retained by its new owners but a new crew sometimes chose another.

Some of the groups had excellent artists within their ranks, as can be seen from this shot of the *Flying Jackass* of the 491st, with the illustration showing the ten crew members astride a donkey. The aircraft's serial number was 44-40239.

The 446th Bomb Group's 42-50882 from Bungay expresses the thoughts of many of its young men in its title *The Wolf Patrol*.

Some of the aircraft's names had particular meanings for the crew as, no doubt, did *Big Chief lil' Beaver*, which was 42-51514 of the 458th from Horsham St Faith.

Pete the POM Inspector 2nd was a B-24D, 42-40370, converted from a bombing role to a brightly coloured assembly ship for the 467th Bomb Group based at Rackheath, Norfolk. Large yellow circles with red outlines covered the aircraft's olive drab colour scheme with the large letter 'P' group symbol being illuminated by light bulbs. The aircraft passed through Warton while serving with another unit.

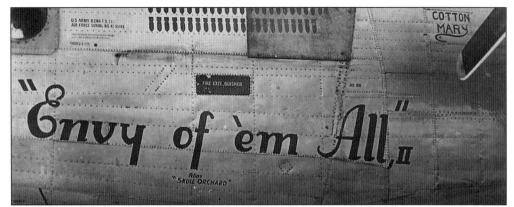

After completing seventy-three missions, the 458th's 42-95108 *Envy of 'em All* II returned to the United States in 1945 only to face the scrap-man.

The 34th's Mendlesham-based *Cokey Flo* arrived at Warton for reassignment to another group when its original unit started to receive B-17s in August 1944. Eight balls neatly cover her assets!

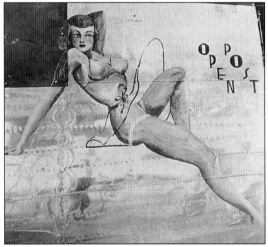

The Horsham St Faith's 458th Bomb Group was the owner of *Open Post*. Once again, the name only meant something to the crew but in an interesting style of lettering, the two 'O's are painted in the red and white group colours, as on the tails of their B-24s.

Shazam of the 458th was painted for the American cartoon hero Captain Marvel, with the name for the word he used to turn him from an ordinary citizen into a crime fighter!

The Lavenham artist of the 487th Bomb Group was one of the most prolific, as he was loaned out to other units as his work became widely known. *This Above All* was the name of a Hollywood film of the time and probably a reasonable reason for the artwork.

The first 466th Bomb Group *Liberty Belle* crashed on take-off from Horsham St Faith on 1 September 1944 while flying as deputy lead with the 458th Bomb Group. This aircraft is thought to be the replacement.

An excellent panoramic view of Warton taken in 1974 shows the proximity of the airfield to the River Ribble and how the main runway extensions go beyond the wartime boundaries. In the left foreground are the remains of Site 12, while to the bottom right of the photograph new houses have been built in the area of Site 11. Further towards the warehouses to the right of the main runway are bases of the Nissen Huts which stood on Site 10. The airfield, now owned by BAE Systems, is still a leader in aeronautical engineering, just as it was in the days of the Second World War.